TUNISIAN
CROCHET
WORKSHOP

To my beautiful granny Thelma for
patiently teaching me all she knew and
inspiring my lifelong passion for crochet.
I think of you with every stitch I make.

TUNISIAN CROCHET WORKSHOP

The complete guide to modern
Tunisian crochet stitches,
techniques and patterns

Michelle Robinson

DAVID & CHARLES

www.davidandcharles.com

CONTENTS

INTRODUCTION

Tunisian crochet has been around for some time but has often been overlooked as the poor cousin to crochet or knitting. In recent times, however, it has been enjoying a modern revival and I couldn't be more delighted to have this opportunity to bring an old craft to you in a new way.

This book is designed to be used by everyone – for the complete novice I suggest you start at the beginning. As you work through the pages you will learn everything you need to know to begin your Tunisian crochet journey from the equipment you need, to basic stitches and techniques, to some more detailed stitch patterns and projects. For those of you that already know the basics of Tunisian crochet, this book can be used as a handy reference guide to techniques and stitch patterns as well as suggesting new projects to try.

All of the projects have been designed to include a broad range of the stitches and techniques shown within the book to give you the opportunity to practice these skills as well as creating beautiful finished items.

I hope as you flick through the pages you will be inspired to pick up your Tunisian hook and hopefully a new passion will be ignited as you discover all the possibilities Tunisian crochet has to offer.

Happy hooking,

Michelle

ABOUT TUNISIAN CROCHET

Often referred to as a fusion between knitting and crochet, Tunisian crochet produces a unique, woven-like fabric. Traditionally used to create thicker items such as blankets, it is also known as Afghan crochet.

Some stitches are unique to Tunisian crochet, yet crocheters and knitters alike will find similarities in the way some stitches are formed.

For example, crocheters will recognise stitches such as Double Crochet and Treble Crochet which are worked in exactly the same way as regular crochet except for the insertion point. Similarly, knitters will recognise stitches such as Tunisian Knit and Purl stitches. While not worked exactly the same way as in knitting, there are similarities in the principles of the stitches and certainly in the look of the finished stitch.

The key differences with Tunisian crochet compared to crochet are:

The work is never turned and you will always be working with the right side facing you.

Rows are worked in two stages: The first stage, the Forward pass, in which stitches are picked up and the loops are left on the hook. The second stage, the Return (or reverse) pass, is where the loops are linked together with a chain stitch as they are dropped back off the hook.

A long hook with a stopper or a cable is required to accommodate the loops being left on the hook. However if you are only making a small piece of Tunisian crochet, you can do this with a regular crochet hook.

A larger hook size is used than the one normally recommended for a particular yarn weight, to accommodate for the thicker fabric that Tunisian crochet produces.

The back of Tunisian crochet fabric has a different appearance than the front. Unlike regular crochet where the back of the fabric is very similar, Tunisian crochet stitches create small bumps at the back of your work, much like the back of knitted Stockinette stitch.

THE ESSENTIALS

Starting from the very beginning...

This section covers everything you need to know before you even pick up your Tunisian crochet hook.

It will introduce you to the tools you need and the different types of yarn – the fundamentals for any crochet project.

TOOLS AND EQUIPMENT

1. RIGID TUNISIAN HOOK

Generally around 30-35cm (12-14in) in length with a hook at one end and a stopper at the other end, this type of hook is the most commonly available. This type of hook is not suitable for projects that require a lot of stitches such as a blanket or shawl.

2. INTERCHANGEABLE HOOK

These hooks are the same length as a regular crochet hook with a fastening device at one end for attaching a cable. This can screw in to the hook or snap on, depending on the manufacturer. You will need to purchase a cable separately (item 3).

3. INTERCHANGEABLE CABLE

These cables are used with interchangeable crochet hooks. They come with a tightening tool and detachable stoppers and can be connected together to make various lengths as required.

4. HOOK WITH FIXED CABLE (NOT SHOWN)

Similar to an interchangeable hook except that the cable is fixed and you are restricted to that length.

5. DOUBLE-ENDED HOOK

Used for working in the round. These come in two different lengths of around 15cm (6in) or 30-35cm (12-14in). Be careful when purchasing a double-ended hook as some are sold with different sized hooks at each end. These are not intended for Tunisian crochet in the round but are sold as versatile regular crochet hooks containing 2 sizes in one hook.

6. DOUBLE-ENDED HOOK CONVERTER

Using two interchangeable hooks in the same size (item 2) and this connector, you can convert your hook into a double-ended hook. Once connected it will measure around 30cm (12in), so can be used for smaller and larger projects.

7. CROCHET HOOK

As long as it doesn't have a handle and preferably without a thumb grip, you can use a regular crochet hook for Tunisian crochet that requires only a few stitches worked at a time, such as Entrelac. You can use a rubber band to keep your stitches from falling off the end.

8. PINS

Used for pinning out your work when blocking. Make sure they are rust proof so as not to stain your work.

9. BLOCKING BOARD (NOT SHOWN)

Interconnecting foam boards found in toy shops or hardware stores are ideal for using as blocking boards.

10. HOOK AND STITCH GAUGE TOOL

Used for measuring stitch and row counts and checking hook size.

11. WOOL TAPESTRY NEEDLE

Used for weaving in ends and joining pieces together. Best with a large eye and fairly blunt point.

12. YARN BOBBINS

For projects that use several colours at the same time such as intarsia, to keep yarn manageable.

13. STITCH MARKERS

Used to mark stitches such as the start or end of a round, a pattern repeat, stitch positioning or short row.

14. CABLE NEEDLE

Used for holding stitches at the front or back of work when making cables.

15. TAPE MEASURE

Indispensable for checking measurements.

16. SCISSORS

Small sharp scissors for cutting yarn.

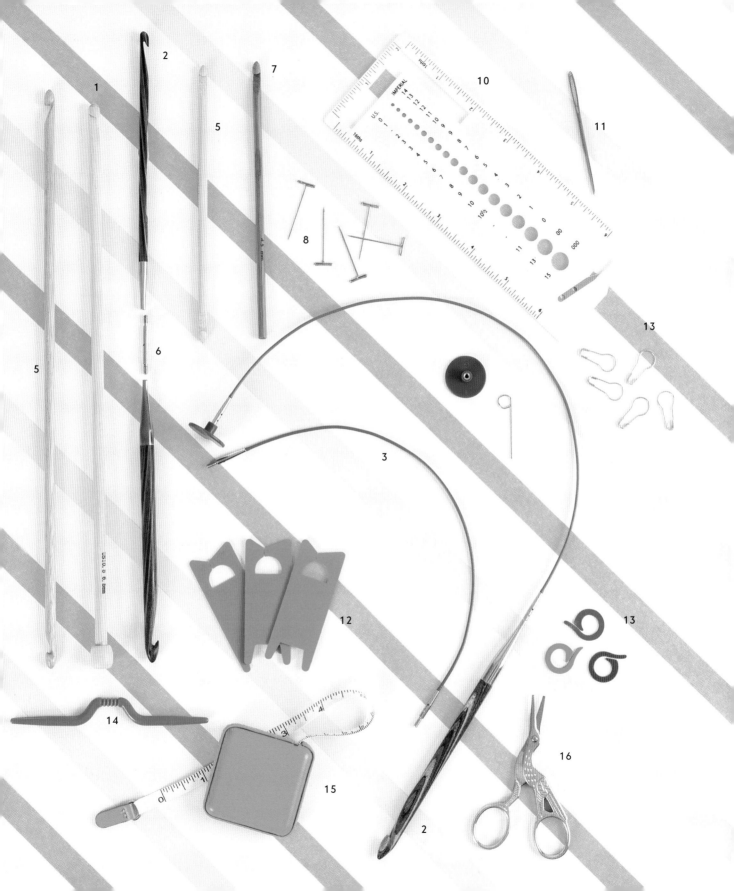

YARN AND HOOK SIZE

There is a huge array of yarns to choose from in today's market and all are suitable for Tunisian crochet.

Amazing results can be produced from the finest of lace weight yarns to the chunkiest of wool roving yarns, or even from unexpected yarn types such as fabric, wire or kitchen string.

Have fun experimenting and let your imagination run wild!

When choosing a yarn for your project, you will need to know the yarn weight in order to choose the correct hook size.

'Yarn weight' refers to the thickness of the thread, not the weight of the ball or the actual thread itself.

If you are unsure of your yarn weight, the best way to determine this is to test the 'wraps per inch' (WPI).

To test for WPI, wrap yarn evenly around a ruler (it doesn't matter how wide it is) for 2.5cm (1in).

Count how many times the yarn is wrapped within this measure then refer to the table below for the approximate yarn weight.

It is important to note that these figures are an approximation only, as yarn weights can vary between brands as well as with each individual's winding tension. So, your results should be used as a starting guide when choosing your yarn before also checking with a gauge swatch to match the pattern's requirements.

Because of the dense fabric Tunisian crochet creates, and also because of the nature of the stitch structure, it is normally recommended that you go up 1-2 sizes in hook size than recommended for a particular yarn weight.

Choosing the correct hook size will also help eliminate some of the curl inherent with Tunisian crochet.

When choosing the right hook for your yarn, if you are working from a pattern always start with the stated hook size as the designer will have chosen the size according to the desired end result eg. the amount of drape needed. Bear in mind that you may still need to adjust your hook size to match the recommended gauge.

If you are not sure which hook size to use then use the table below as a guide. Start with the larger of the suggested sizes first, but if you find that your stitches are too loose then try again with the smaller size.

NOTE

IF YOU NEED TO PURCHASE A TUNISIAN HOOK FOR A PROJECT, YOU CAN TEST FOR THE CORRECT HOOK SIZE WITH A FEW STITCHES ON A REGULAR CROCHET HOOK BEFORE COMMITTING TO BUYING THE TUNISIAN HOOK.

UK/AUS/NZ YARN WEIGHT	US YARN WEIGHT	WPI (WRAPS PER INCH)	SUGGESTED TUNISIAN HOOK SIZE (SEE NOTE)
2 ply	Laceweight	18+	3–5 mm
3–4 ply	Fingering/Sock	14–18	3.5–5 mm
5 ply	Sport	12–14	4–5 mm
8 ply/DK	Light Worsted	11–12	5–7 mm
10ply/Aran	Worsted	8-9	7–9 mm
12 ply/Chunky	Bulky	7	9–11 mm
14 ply/Super Chunky	Super Bulky	5–6	10 mm+

CHOOSING COLOURS

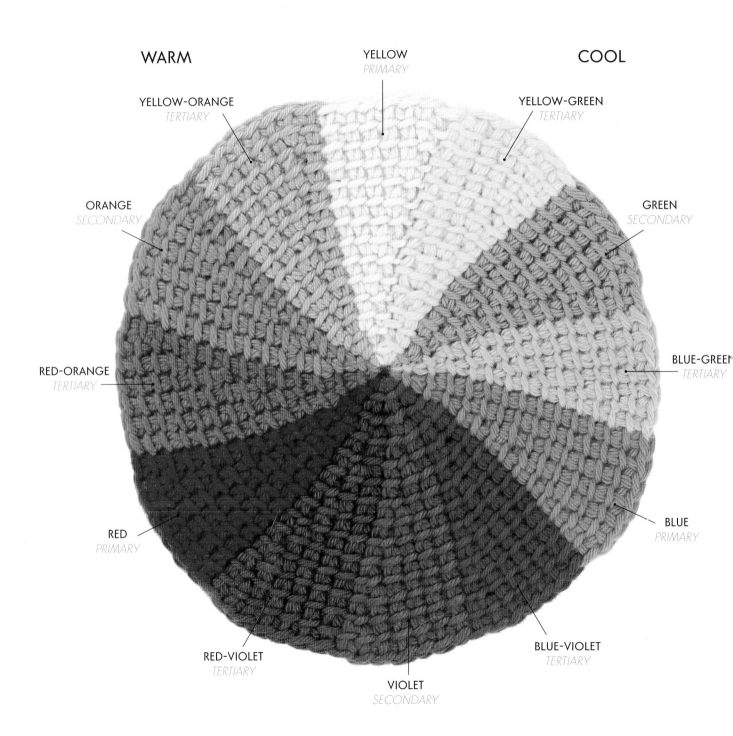

WARM

COOL

YELLOW
PRIMARY

YELLOW-ORANGE
TERTIARY

YELLOW-GREEN
TERTIARY

ORANGE
SECONDARY

GREEN
SECONDARY

RED-ORANGE
TERTIARY

BLUE-GREEN
TERTIARY

RED
PRIMARY

BLUE
PRIMARY

RED-VIOLET
TERTIARY

BLUE-VIOLET
TERTIARY

VIOLET
SECONDARY

Choosing colours is an important step when starting a new project. Your choices will have a huge impact on the finished look and even the smallest change in colours can make a dramatic difference to the overall look of the finished project. This need not make choosing colour intimidating though. With this introduction to colour theory, choosing colours for your next project can become an enjoyable experience.

Colour combinations can be found everywhere around us. Look around and notice attractive colour combinations in nature, art, homewares or even clothing. Keep a journal of colour combinations that please you for future reference.

The internet is also a valuable source of inspiration with many sites that have already created beautiful colour combinations for you.

The most useful tool you can have though, is a basic knowledge of the colour wheel and a few simple colour matching guides. Following are the basic colour matching guides, all tried and true formulas. All work well in their own way but a good place to start when choosing your colour scheme would be the Triad, as it produces a pleasing and harmonious set of colours that are hard to get wrong.

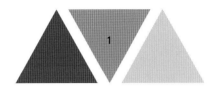

1. MONOCHROMATIC

• Various shades of the same colour

• Adds depth and visual interest when working with just one colour

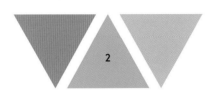

2. ANALOGOUS

• Colours adjacent to each other on the colour wheel

• Low contrast

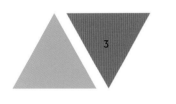

3. COMPLEMENTARY

• Opposite sides of the colour wheel

• These colours used together create high contrast

4. SPLIT COMPLEMENTARY

• Start with a base colour then choose two colours adjacent to its complement

5. TRIAD

• Three colours equally spaced around wheel

• Harmonious combination

GAUGE

Gauge is the number of stitches and rows per cm in a piece of crochet or knitting. The number of stitches is affected by various factors such as yarn weight, hook size and whether you are a tight or loose stitcher.

All of these factors will affect the finished size of your project. Checking your gauge is an important first step if you want to match the gauge used in a pattern or you are substituting with a different yarn and want to ensure it matches the designer's yarn choice as closely as possible.

While it's not crucial to match gauge exactly for items such as blankets, where a few centimetres difference will not affect your finished project, it is important to match gauge when making garments or items that are required to fit a certain measurement.

The first step in checking your gauge is to make a swatch in your chosen yarn, using the same hook size as stated in the pattern.

Gauge is usually measured over a 10x10cm (4x4in) square, but to get an accurate stitch count your swatch needs to be bigger than this. Therefore your swatch should measure at least 15x15cm (6x6in) and be worked using the same stitch as used in the pattern.

It is also important to note if the pattern states whether the gauge was checked before or after blocking. This will affect your final stitch count so do the same as stated in the pattern.

Lay your swatch on a flat surface. There are two different ways to mark out the area to be measured. You can either use a ruler or tape measure, or a gauge tool if you have one, see Tools and Equipment chapter.

If you are using a tape measure or ruler, lay it over the swatch and use pins to mark out a 10cm (4in) square.

If you are using a gauge tool place this over the top of your swatch, making sure that it is held straight and lined up at the start of a stitch and row.

Count exactly how many stitches and rows are within this square. This may mean that you will be counting partial stitches or rows. It is very important that these are also included in the overall count.

Compare your gauge to the pattern. If it is exactly the same then you don't need to make any changes and you are ready to begin. However, if yours does not match then some adjustments need to be made.

If you have:

• More stitches or rows: This may mean you are a tight stitcher. Increase your hook size – go up one hook size and re-measure until you have matched gauge.

• Fewer stitches or rows: This may mean you are a loose stitcher. Decrease your hook size – go down one hook size and re-measure until you have matched gauge.

READING PATTERNS AND CHARTS

WRITTEN PATTERNS

Tunisian crochet patterns are written in the same style as regular crochet patterns, but with a whole new set of stitch abbreviations to get used to.

The first step to approaching any pattern is to read through it entirely before you break out your hook and yarn.

Don't worry if it doesn't all make sense at first, some of the instructions will be clearer once you are actually making the project. The most important things to look out for are:

TERMS

Regular crochet patterns can be written in either US or UK/Aus terminology. This can be confusing to even the most experienced crocheter, especially if it hasn't been made clear what terminology has been used. If unsure of the terminology used, look out for 'single crochet' or 'half double crochet' as these are both exclusive to US terms.

Unlike with regular crochet patterns, Tunisian crochet uses the same international language for stitch names. However, as some Tunisian crochet patterns may also include crochet elements, it is important to understand which terminology has been used.

All the projects in this book have been written in US terms.

YARN AND OTHER MATERIALS

Check you have all the materials needed before beginning your project. There is nothing more frustrating than not having enough yarn to finish a project, especially if you are unable to get any more in the same dye lot or if it has been discontinued.

GAUGE AND SIZE

Matching the designer's gauge isn't essential if you are making a non-fitted item, but if you are making an item that must be a specific size then it is important that you match the gauge. Read more about this in the preceding chapter on Gauge.

ABBREVIATIONS

Tunisian crochet patterns contain some familiar crochet abbreviations such as 'ch' for chain but there are also many new abbreviations to familiarise yourself with. There is no need to memorise every Tunisian crochet stitch abbreviation. As you begin working from Tunisian crochet patterns, you will quickly start to become familiar with the common stitch abbreviations such as Tss, which is used for Tunisian Simple Stitch. Refer to the abbreviations guide in the Glossary as you come across unfamiliar abbreviations. With practice, reading Tunisian patterns will become second nature.

SPECIAL STITCHES AND TECHNIQUES

If a special stitch or technique has been used in a pattern, the instructions will be written here together with its abbreviation. It's a good idea to practice the stitch or technique before starting your project to get a feel for it. Once you begin working from the pattern and come across the abbreviation, refer back to this section for the instructions if a refresher is needed.

CHARTS

You will come across two types of charts in Tunisian crochet – symbol charts and colourwork charts. Both are very easy to use once you understand how to read them and you may find that you actually prefer them to written instructions.

SYMBOL CHARTS

Unlike crochet symbol charts, which resemble the finished item, Tunisian crochet charts are more like knitting charts. These charts use symbols to represent stitches or a pattern repeat and are easy to glance at when working on a pattern to see which stitch to use next, rather than reading through the words in a written pattern. You can also use both in conjunction with each other, referring to the symbol chart if you are unsure of the written instructions given or vice versa.

Unfortunately, with the exception of a few, the symbols are not universally standard, so they may vary from designer to designer and you should refer to their symbol key when working from a pattern.

For a key to the symbols used in this book, please refer to the Symbol Chart (see Glossary).

HOW TO READ A SYMBOL CHART

Tunisian symbol charts are read from bottom to top and each row is read starting from right to left.

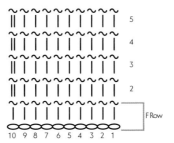

Each row contains symbols for both the forward pass (they differ depending on the stitch used), and the return pass, which is notated with ∿ symbols across the top of the row.

COLOURWORK CHARTS

When working any colourwork pattern, whether it is intarsia or stranded, you will most likely work from a colourwork chart. These charts show the design clearly and working from them makes it easy to see where the colour change occurs and how many stitches to work in each colour.

Colourwork patterns will usually start off with written instructions to set up your project with the foundation row. They will then direct you to work from the chart for the remainder.

HOW TO READ A COLOURWORK CHART

Colourwork charts are fairly self-explanatory and will either show the complete design, or they may show only the pattern repeat section for designs where the same pattern is repeated several times.

Charts are read from bottom to top and rows are read from right to left.

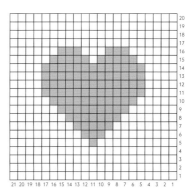

HOLDING THE HOOK AND YARN

Picking up a long Tunisian crochet hook for the first time may feel a little foreign in your hand and you may find that the way you normally hold your crochet hook might not be suitable for Tunisian crochet.

Because of the stitches being kept on the hook, the different motion of Tunisian crochet and the difference in hook size, you will find it more effective to hold the hook in an overhand grip similar to a knife grip:

• Using your dominant hand, hold hook with your hand placed over the top as you would a knife with the end resting lightly on your 3rd and 4th fingers.

• Use your index finger and thumb to control the hook as you slide through the stitches.

The key to creating neat work is to achieve an even tension. The way you hold your yarn is the main factor controlling your tension.

There are many ways to hold your yarn and there is no right or wrong way. As long as you are comfortable with your method and maintain an even and consistent tension then that is the main thing.

If you are already a crocheter and have a preferred way then continue to hold your yarn the same way for Tunisian crochet.

If you are picking up a hook and yarn for the first time, begin by following these steps. At first it may feel awkward but with practice it will soon become second nature.

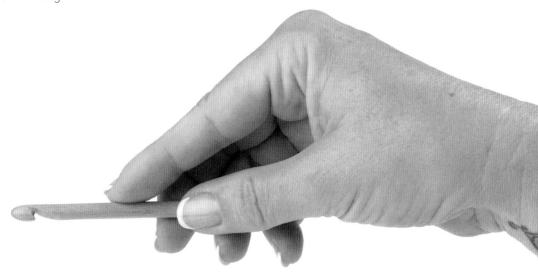

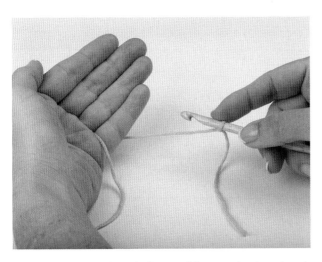

Wrap yarn around the little finger of the non-dominant hand,

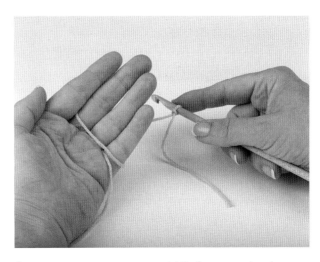

then pass yarn over your two middle fingers and under your index finger,

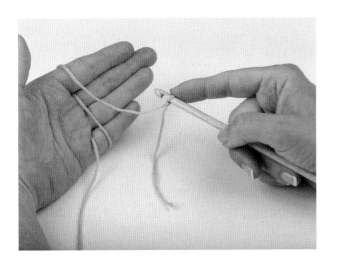

then over your index finger.

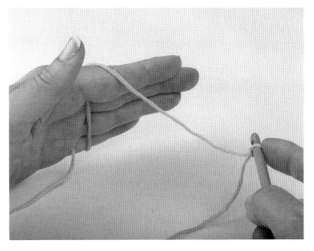

The index finger will be used to position the yarn and your tension will be controlled by how tightly you hold the yarn in the other three fingers.

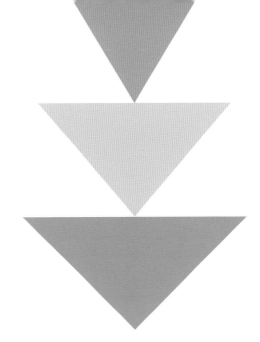

THE BASICS

Now that we have covered the essentials, it's time to pick up your hook and learn the basics of Tunisian crochet.

We'll practice lots of stitches so that you have a library of swatches to refer to when you move onto making projects.

GETTING STARTED

To begin, we will work a small practice swatch of the five basic Tunisian stitches, starting with the most commonly used stitch, the Tunisian Simple stitch. We will then progress on to Tunisian Purl stitch, Tunisian Knit stitch, Tunisian Reverse stitch and Tunisian Full stitch.

These five basic stitches form the basis of most stitch patterns. Once you have mastered these you will be ready to tackle any stitch pattern with confidence.

FOUNDATION ROW

Tunisian crochet always begins with a foundation row. The foundation row consists of a starting chain and a base row of stitches, which are then used as an insertion point for the next row of stitches.

This foundation row is always worked the same way regardless of the stitch pattern being used.

To create a row of Tunisian crochet stitches, two stages are required. These stages are known as:

1. Forward pass – where you will pick up loops onto the hook, leaving them all there until the next stage.

2. Return pass – where you will link the stitches together as you drop them back off the hook. The return pass is almost always worked the same way. Unless otherwise stated within a pattern you will work the return pass as described below.

Your work is never turned in Tunisian crochet and you will always have the right side of the fabric facing you. If you are right handed you will always be working from right to left on the forward pass and if you are left handed you will be working from left to right.

FORWARD PASS

Chain 20 (or desired number of stitches). Try and keep your chain fairly loose but not so loose as to become distorted. This is important, as if your chain is too tight it will be almost impossible to insert your hook into it in the next step.

Roll your chain slightly towards you, and starting in the 2nd ch from hook, insert the hook into the back bump that lies behind the chain. (Please note that the photo shows the second stitch worked, into 3rd ch from hook.)

Yarn over hook and pull through a loop, leaving loop on hook. (The photo shows that after working 2 stitches you have 3 loops on hook.)

Continue picking up loops this way until you've reached the end of the chain (20 loops on hook). You have now completed the forward pass of the foundation row and will have the same number of loops on your hook as you had in your initial chain.

RETURN PASS

Don't turn – you will now be working left to right if you are right handed or right to left if you are left handed.

Yarn over hook and pull through the first loop on hook.

This 'ch 1' now becomes your 'locking' chain which will link your stitches together as you drop them back off your hook as follows:

*Yarn over hook and pull through the next 2 loops on hook. Repeat from * until there is one loop remaining on your hook. Return pass completed. The stitch remaining on the hook will now become the first stitch of the next row.

Now that you have completed a foundation row you are ready to begin working your stitch pattern.

For this exercise, before we move on to learning the basic stitches, we'll take a moment to look at the anatomy of Tunisian crochet which will make it easier to understand some of the terminology and how it all works.

Once you are familiar with the anatomy of Tunisian crochet, practice at least 5 rows of each of the basic stitches in the following chapter on your swatch to get a feel for how each stitch is formed.

ANATOMY OF TUNISIAN CROCHET

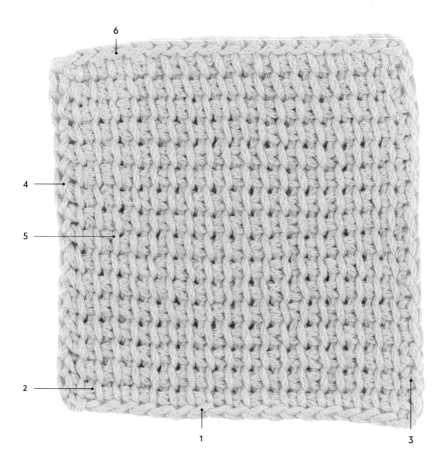

1. FOUNDATION CHAIN
Loops are picked up from the back bump of the foundation chain.

2. FOUNDATION ROW
The first row of stitches will always be created the same way regardless of stitch pattern.

3. FIRST STITCH
The first stitch of a row is not worked into and always remains the same regardless of the stitch pattern.

4. END ST
The last stitch of a row will always be worked the same regardless of the stitch pattern.

5. ROWS
Each vertical bar represents one row.

6. BIND OFF
Stitches are bound off with a slip stitch.

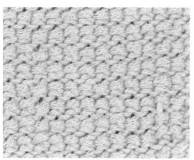

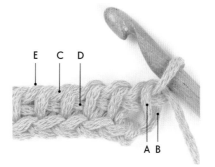

A. Front vertical bar

B. Back vertical bar

C. Horizontal chain – top strand

D. Horizontal chain – bottom strand

E. Horizontal chain – back bump

TAMING THE CURL

How do I stop my Tunisian crochet from curling? This is the most common complaint about Tunisian crochet and a question I get asked most often.

Tunisian crochet curls because in many of the stitches the bulk of the stitch lies at the back of the work, causing the fabric to be heavier at the back than the front, thus creating an unequal tension and pulling the work in.

Some stitches, such as simple stitch and especially the knit stitch, will curl more than others as they have a flat, smooth front with a bumpy back. However stitches such as purl or reverse stitch have a bump on both the front and back of the fabric, causing the tension to even out somewhat.

The good news is that the curl can be tamed quite easily. My top two favourite methods are to use an extended stitch in the foundation row and blocking.

Try out some of these methods for yourself and notice the difference they make:

EXTENDED STITCH

This is my favourite method of controlling the curl. It is almost undetectable and blends in nicely with the remainder of your work. As with all methods, it will still benefit from blocking but will not need very much taming.

When picking up loops in your foundation row, add a ch 1 after you pick up the loop (extended stitch).

BLOCKING

Blocking really does help in taming the curl. Blocking works by settling the stitches into place, causing the fabric to relax and straighten out (see Blocking for different methods).

BIGGER HOOK

When working Tunisian crochet, it's generally recommended to use a hook 1–2 sizes larger than recommended for your yarn weight. Using a bigger hook can help by making your stitches looser, but you will most likely still have some curl and still need to block your work.

LOOSE TENSION

It's important to try to keep your beginning chain and stitches fairly loose with Tunisian crochet. Too tight stitches will cause your work to curl more than a looser stitch. There will still be some curl and your work will still need to be blocked.

PURL STITCH OR REVERSE STITCH

Working a row or two of Purl or Reverse stitch at the beginning of your work will help to reduce the curl but it will create an obvious row of 'bumpy' stitches that may not blend in with the rest of your work.

CROCHET BORDER

Adding a border of regular crochet in conjunction with blocking works well to tame the curl and can also become a design feature.

BASIC STITCHES

NOTE

THE LAST STITCH ON A FORWARD PASS IS ALWAYS WORKED THE SAME WAY REGARDLESS OF THE STITCH BEING USED AND WILL BE REFERRED TO FROM HERE AS 'WORK END ST'.

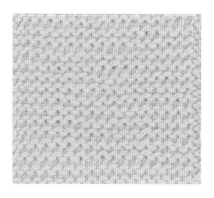

TUNISIAN SIMPLE STITCH (TSS)

• Also known as 'Afghan stitch' or 'Basic stitch'

• Has a tendency to curl

Forward: Skip 1st vertical bar, insert hook from right to left under 2nd vertical bar, yo and pull up loop, keeping loop on hook. Continue picking up loops this way until you reach the last st. Insert hook under the last vertical bar and the bar that lies directly behind it (2 bars on hook), yo and pull up loop - end st made (see Note).

Return: Yo, pull through 1 loop, *yo pull through 2 loops. Repeat from * to end (1 loop left on hook).

TUNISIAN PURL STITCH (TPS)

• Looks similar to knitted purl stitch

• Has less tendency to curl

Forward: Skip 1st vertical bar, *bring yarn forward to front of work, insert hook from right to left under next vertical bar, bring yarn across the front of vertical bar and to back of work, yo and pull up a loop. Repeat from * to last st, work end st.

Return: As for Tunisian Simple Stitch.

Forward: Working from the back of your work, skip 1st vertical bar, *insert hook under the vertical bar of the next stitch at the back of your work, yo, pull up loop. Repeat from * to last st, work end st.

Return: As for Tunisian Simple Stitch.

TUNISIAN KNIT STITCH (TKS)

TUNISIAN REVERSE STITCH (TRS)

• Looks similar to knitted stocking stitch

• Creates a thick fabric

• Has a tendency to curl

Forward: Skip 1st vertical bar, *insert hook from front to back between the front and back vertical bars of the next stitch, yo and pull up loop. Repeat from * into each st up to last st, work end st.

Return: As for Tunisian Simple Stitch.

• Worked just like a Tunisian Simple Stitch but instead, it is worked through the back vertical bar situated behind your work

• Stitch forms horizontal bumps similar to Tunisian Purl stitch and can be used as a replacement for this stitch

• Has less tendency to curl

Row 1 – Forward: Insert hook into sp between 2nd and 3rd vertical bars and into each sp between sts to last st, work end st.

Return: As for Tunisian Simple Stitch.

Row 2 – Forward: Insert hook into sp between 1st and 2nd vertical bars and into each sp between sts up to last sp, sk this sp, work end st.

Return: As for Tunisian Simple Stitch. Repeat Rows 1 and 2 to form pattern.

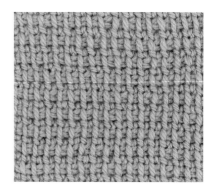

TUNISIAN FULL STITCH (TFS)

• Worked on its own, this stitch is called a Tunisian Full stitch and can be used to increase stitches (Make 1) or for working into a space between stitches or a 'yarn over' space such as an eyelet

• When rows of Tunisian Full stitch are made it then becomes known as either Mesh Stitch or Gobelin Stitch which is a 2 row pattern repeat with staggered starting and end points to prevent work from biasing

• The following instructions are for working in rows (Mesh Stitch)

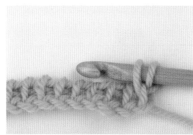

TUNISIAN EXTENDED STITCH (TES)

• Instructions are given for a Tunisian Extended Simple Stitch, however you can extend almost any stitch by adding a 'ch 1' at the end of each stitch

• When you come across this stitch in a pattern, be sure to take note of where to insert your hook as this may vary from pattern to pattern

• The extra height of extended stitches helps to eliminate curl and is a good alternative stitch to use for your foundation row

• This stitch has a slightly raised texture and more stretch than regular stitches, making it ideal for garments or projects where a drapey effect is required

• To accommodate the extra stitch height, a chain stitch is added at the start and end of each row

Forward: Ch 1, *insert hook under next vertical bar, yo pull up loop, ch 1. Repeat from * to last st, work end st, ch 1 (this is additional to the first ch 1 of the return).

Return: As for Tunisian Simple Stitch.

To make an Extended Stitch

Foundation row: Ch desired number plus 1, insert into the back bump of 3rd ch from hook, *yo and pull up a loop, ch 1 (this counts as first st + ch 1). Repeat from * in each ch to end leaving all loops on hook. Return.

TUNISIAN DOUBLE CROCHET (TDC)

• This stitch is also known as Tunisian Double Stitch (Tds)

• It is worked almost the same as a regular Double Crochet stitch

• To accommodate the extra stitch height, a chain stitch is added at the start of each row

Forward: Ch 1, *yo, insert hook under next vertical bar, yo pull up loop, yo, pull through 2 loops. Repeat from * to last st, work end st.

Return: As for Tunisian Simple Stitch.

BIND OFF

Although this step is not necessary to hold your stitches in place after finishing your piece, binding off will give your work a neat finished edge.

To bind off you will be working a slip stitch, dropping stitches off as you go.

After you have completed the return pass on the last row, insert hook in next stitch as per the stitch type you were last working i.e. if you were working in Tss then you would insert hook Tss-wise, yo and pull loop through both loops on hook.

Repeat for each stitch until one loop remains. Cut yarn and draw through loop to tie off.

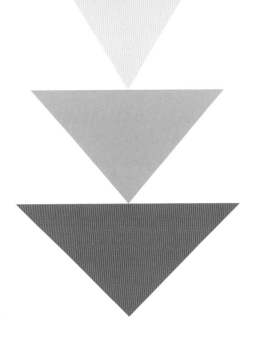

BEYOND THE BASICS

Now that you are feeling confident in the basics of Tunisian crochet, this section is designed to help you to develop and expand your new-found skills.

We'll look at lots of different stitches and make some more swatches – sew these together once they're done and you could make a cushion cover!

COLOURWORK

Colourwork falls into two distinct categories, Intarsia and Stranded. Both create patterns in your work but are worked differently to each other and each serves a different purpose.

Both styles of colourwork are usually worked from a chart which makes it easy to see where colour changes are to be made (see Reading Patterns and Charts).

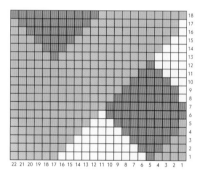

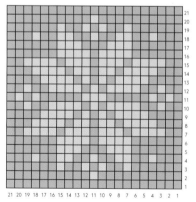

INTARSIA

Intarsia is used to create patterns or pictures with multiple colours or for large areas of single colour where it is not practical to carry the unused colour across the back of your work.

A separate bobbin for each colour is used with only one colour used at a time, while the inactive colour is left hanging until the next colour change.

Before you begin, refer to Change Colour – Mid Row in the Changing Colour section.

To begin, wind yarn onto bobbins for each separate area of colour. If the same colour appears twice (or more) in each row then a separate bobbin for each area of colour will be needed.

Using the first colour on the chart design, work the required number of stitches.

Change to the next colour, wrapping the working end of the new colour under the previous colour. Drop the first colour and continue working in new colour for the required number of stitches. Return as normal, changing colours as they appear.

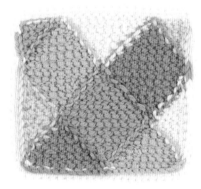

STRANDED COLOURWORK

Often referred to as Fair Isle in knitting, this style of colourwork is used to create small repeating patterns, usually using only two colours at a time. The unused colour is carried behind the work, creating 'floats' of yarn, and creates a thicker fabric due to the carried yarn.

Stranded colourwork is best worked in Tunisian knit stitch as it gives width to each stitch, creating a more realistic representation of the design, however it can also be worked in Tunisian simple stitch, which will result in a narrower design.

Before you begin, refer to Change Colour – Mid Row in the Changing Colour section.

NOTE

ANOTHER WAY TO ADD COLOURWORK TO YOUR PROJECTS IS TO ADD A DESIGN WITH DUPLICATE STITCH (SEE EMBELLISHMENT).

HOW TO CARRY (FLOAT) YARN

It is important to keep the tension of the unused yarn loose as it is carried across the back of your work. Ideally, you should be able to insert the tip of your little finger under the carried loop of yarn.

You also don't want long stretches of unused yarn running behind your work. To avoid this, it is advisable to 'lock your float' every 2-3 stitches or so.

To lock the float, wrap the unused yarn around the working yarn before continuing, making sure it is not pulled too tight. This locks the unused yarn in place and should appear as a small loop at the back of your work.

Using the first colour on the chart design, work the required amount of stitches.

Change to the next colour, wrapping the working end of the new colour under the previous colour, and continue working in the new colour, carrying the unused yarn behind your work and locking the float every 2-3 stitches.

Return as normal, changing colours as they appear and locking floats the same way as in the forward pass.

CHANGING COLOUR

CHANGE COLOUR – LEFT EDGE

At the beginning of the return pass, yarn over with new colour and pull through first loop on hook, then continue return pass as usual with the new colour.

CHANGE COLOUR – RIGHT EDGE

On the final 2 loops of the return pass in the row before you wish to change colour, yarn over with the new colour and pull through the last 2 loops (one loop left on hook in new colour). Continue working next forward pass in new colour.

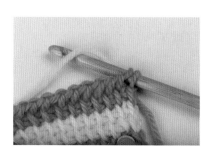

CHANGE COLOUR – MID ROW

This type of colour change will be used in both intarsia and stranded colourwork. However, the way that you treat the unused colour differs. Refer to the instructions relevant to the type of colourwork you are doing.

On the forward pass, work up to the point where a colour change is required, insert hook in next st, yo in new colour, work required number of stitches in new colour.

On the return pass, work as normal until there is one loop of the contrast colour left on the hook, yo in new colour and continue return pass as usual.

CARRY YARN UP SIDE OF WORK

When working in stripes, instead of cutting the unused colour each time, you can carry it up the side of your piece by wrapping the unused colour over the top of the working colour before completing the next stitch. This draws the unused yarn up a row and locks it into place.

BUILD YOUR
STITCH REPERTOIRE

HONEYCOMB STITCH

- Multiples of 2
- 2 row pattern repeat formed with alternating Tss and Tps stitches
- First and last stitches do not form part of pattern and are always worked the same

Stitches Used

Tunisian Simple Stitch (Tss): see Basic Stitches

Tunisian Purl Stitch (Tps): see Basic Stitches

Row 1 (foundation row): Chain required number of stitches. Pick up a loop from back bump in 2nd ch from hook, and in each ch to end, leaving all loops on hook. Return.

Row 2: Starting in 2nd vertical bar, work a Tps (1), work a Tss into next st (2). Continue alternating Tps and Tss up to last st, work end st. Return.

Row 3: This row is worked the same as Row 2 but in the opposite order i.e. you will be working a Tps above the previous Tss and a Tss above the previous Tps.

Starting in 2nd vertical bar, work a Tss, then work a Tps into next st (3). Continue alternating stitches this way up to last st, work end st. Return.

Repeat Rows 2 and 3 to form pattern.

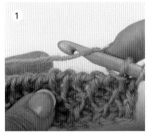

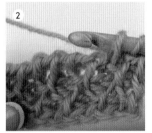

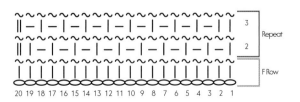

BASKETWEAVE STITCH

- Multiples of 5
- 8 row pattern repeat
- First and last stitches do not form part of pattern and are always worked the same

Stitches Used

Tunisian Knit Stitch (Tks): see Basic Stitches

Tunisian Purl Stitch (Tps): see Basic Stitches

Row 1 (foundation row): Chain required number of stitches. Pick up a loop from back bump in 2nd ch from hook, and in each ch to end, leaving all loops on hook. Return.

Row 2: Tks in next 4 sts, *Tps in next 5 sts, (1) Tks in next 5 sts. Repeat from * to last 5 sts, Tps 4, work end st. Return.

Rows 3-5: Work as for Row 2.

Row 6: Tps in next 4 sts, *Tks in next 5 sts (2), Tps in next 5 sts. Repeat from * to last 5 sts, Tks 4, work end st. Return.

Rows 7-9: Work as for Row 6.

Repeat Rows 2-9 for desired length.

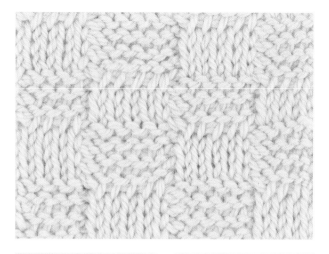

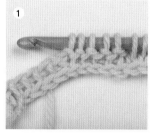

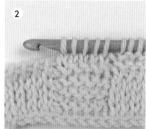

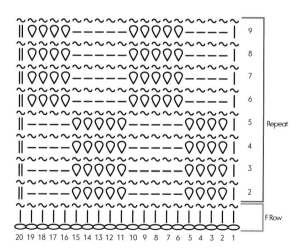

CROSSED STITCH

- Multiples of 2 + 2
- 1 row pattern repeat
- First and last stitches do not form part of pattern and are always worked the same

Stitches Used

Tunisian Simple stitch (Tss): see Basic Stitches

Row 1 (foundation row): Chain required number of stitches. Pick up a loop from back bump in 2nd ch from hook, and in each ch to end, leaving all loops on hook. Return.

Row 2: *Sk next st, Tss 1 (1), Tss in skipped st (2). Repeat from * to last st, work end st. Return.

Repeat Row 2 for desired length.

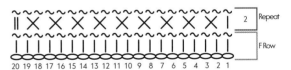

BOBBLE STITCH

• Any number of Tss can be worked between bobbles. This swatch sample has 5 Tss between bobbles

• Multiples: dependent on how many sts required between bobbles + 1 st for bobble + 2 (first and last sts) + number of stitches required to balance pattern. Swatch sample is in multiples of 6 + 2 + 1

• First and last stitches do not form part of pattern and are always worked the same

Stitches Used

Tunisian Simple Stitch (Tss): see Basic Stitches

Row 1 (foundation row): Chain required number of stitches. Pick up a loop from back bump in 2nd ch from hook, and in each ch to end, leaving all loops on hook. Return.

Rows 2-3: Tss to end. Return.

Row 4: Tss 3, [yo, insert hook into next st Tks-wise, yo, pull up lp (1), yo, draw through 2 lps on hook] (2). Repeat 3 more times working into the same st, yo, draw through 4 lps on hook (3), yo, draw through 1 loop on hook (bobble made), *Tss 5, make bobble. Repeat from * to last 4 sts, Tss 3, work end st. Return.

Rows 5-7: Tss to end. Return.

Row 8: Tss 6, make bobble, *Tss 5, make bobble. Repeat from * to last 7 sts, Tss 6, work end st. Return.

Row 9: Tss to end. Return.

Rows 2-9 form the pattern of offset bobbles as shown in the pictured swatch.

To create a continuous pattern as shown in swatch, repeat Rows 2-9 for desired length.

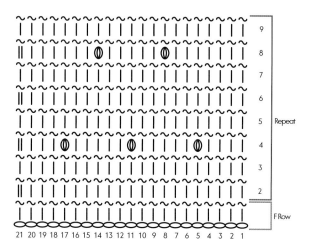

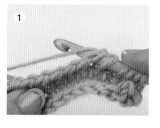

2 X 1 RIB

• Multiples of 3 + 1 (to balance pattern) + 2 (first and last sts)

• First and last stitches do not form part of pattern and are always worked the same

Stitches Used

Tunisian Knit Stitch (Tks): see Basic Stitches

Tunisian Purl Stitch (Tps): see Basic Stitches

Row 1 (foundation row): Chain required number of stitches. Pick up a loop from back bump in 2nd ch from hook, and in each ch to end, leaving all loops on hook. Return.

Row 2: *Tps into next st (1), Tks into next 2 sts (2). Repeat from * to last st, work end st. Return.

Repeat Row 2 for desired length.

NOTE

YOU CAN CREATE ANY RIB COMBINATION DEPENDING ON HOW MANY OF EACH STITCH YOU USE.

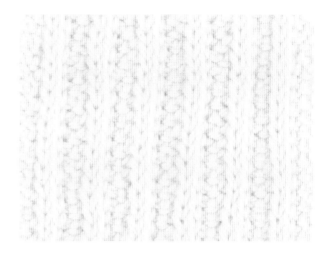

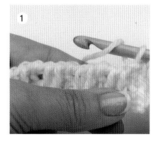

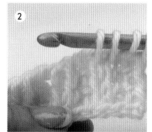

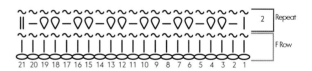

LATTICE STITCH

• Multiple of any odd number

• 2 row pattern repeat

• First and last stitches do not form part of pattern and are always worked the same

Special Stitches and Techniques Used

Tunisian Simple Stitch (Tss): see Basic Stitches

Tss2tog: insert hook under next 2 vertical bars, yo, pull up a loop (1 loop left on hook)

Row 1 (foundation row): Chain required number of stitches. Pick up a loop from back bump in 2nd ch from hook, and in each ch to end, leaving all loops on hook. Return.

Row 2: *Tss2tog (1), Tss back into 1st st of Tss2tog (2). Repeat from * to last 2 sts, Tss 1, work end st. Return.

Row 3: Tss 1, *Tss2tog, Tss back into 1st st of Tss2tog. Repeat from * to last st, work end st. Return.

Rows 2 and 3 form pattern. Repeat for desired length.

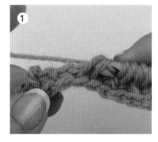

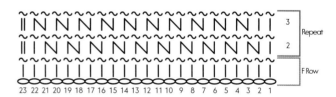

CABLE

- Multiples of 6 + 2
- 5 row pattern repeat
- First and last stitches do not form part of pattern and are always worked the same

Stitches Used

Tunisian Knit Stitch (Tks): see Basic Stitches

Tunisian Purl Stitch (Tps): see Basic Stitches

Other Materials

Cable needle

Row 1 (foundation row): Chain required number of stitches. Pick up a loop from back bump in 2nd ch from hook, and in each ch to end, leaving all loops on hook. Return.

Row 2: Tps 6, Tks 6, Tps 6, work end st. Return.

Row 3: Work as for Row 2.

Row 4: Tps 6, Tks 3, yo, Tks 3, Tps 6 (1), work end st. Return (you will now have one extra stitch on your hook).

Row 5: Tps 6, Tks 3, skip yo sp from previous row, Tks 3, Tps 6, work end st. Return.

Row 6: Tps 6, Tks 3, slip sts just worked onto cable needle and keep at front of work (2), Tks 3, slip sts from cable needle back onto hook, (3), Tks 6, work end st. Return.

Rows 2-6 form pattern. Repeat for desired length.

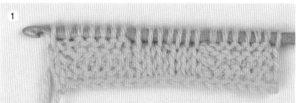

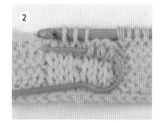
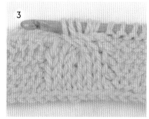

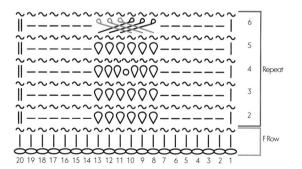

2-TONE TSS

- Multiples of any number
- 2 row pattern repeat
- The 2-tone effect is created by working the forward pass in one colour then the return pass in a contrast colour
- First and last stitches do not form part of pattern and are always worked the same

Stitches Used

Tunisian Simple Stitch (Tss): see Basic Stitches

Row 1 (foundation row): Using Colour **A**, chain required number of stitches. Pick up a loop from back bump in 2nd ch from hook, and in each ch to end, leaving all loops on hook. Return using Colour **B** (1).

Row 2: Continuing with Colour **B**, Tss to last st (2), work end st. Return using Colour **A** (3).

Row 3: Continuing with Colour **A**, Tss to last st, work end st. Return using Colour **B**.

Repeat Rows 2 and 3 for desired length.

NOTE

THIS METHOD OF CHANGING COLOURS ALTERNATELY CAN BE USED WITH ANY STITCH PATTERN.

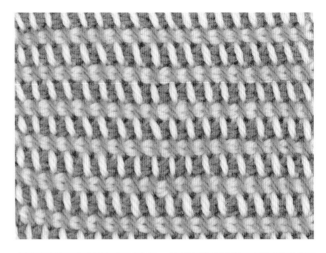

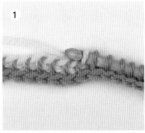

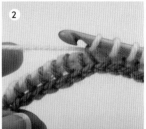

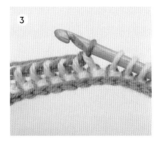

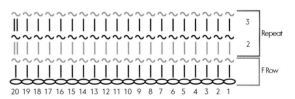

CHEVRON

- Multiples of 12 + 1
- 1 row pattern repeat
- Width of chevrons can be easily adjusted by changing the number of stitches in between increases and decreases
- Change the look by altering the colour rows (see Chevron Cushion for another variation)
- First and last stitches do not form part of pattern and are always worked the same

Special Stitches and Techniques Used

Tunisian Simple Stitch (Tss): see Basic Stitches

Tss3tog: insert hook under next 3 vertical bars, yo, pull up a loop (1 loop left on hook)

M1 (make 1) – top bar: insert hook under top loop of horizontal bar before next st (1), yo, pull up loop and leave on hook

Row 1 (foundation row): Chain required number of stitches. Pick up a loop from back bump in 2nd ch from hook, and in each ch to end, leaving all loops on hook. Return.

Row 2: *M1 (1) Tss 4, Tss3tog (2), Tss 4, M1, Tss 1 Repeat from * to last st, replacing last Tss1 with an end st. Return.

Repeat Row 2 for desired length.

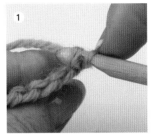

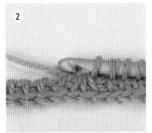

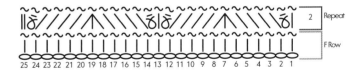

GRID STITCH

- Multiples of 4 + 1
- 4 row pattern repeat
- First and last stitches do not form part of pattern and are always worked the same

Stitches Used

Tunisian Simple Stitch (Tss): see Basic Stitches

Long Tunisian Front Post Double Crochet (LTfpdc): yo, insert hook under front and back strands of vertical bar 2 rows below (1), yo, pull up a lp, yo, pull through 2 lps on hook (1 lp left on hook)

Row 1 (foundation row): Using Colour **A**, chain required number of stitches. Pick up a loop from back bump in 2nd ch from hook, and in each ch to end, leaving all loops on hook. Return, changing to Colour **B** on last 2 lps.

Row 2: Continuing with Colour **B**, work Tss to last st, work end st. Return, changing back to Colour **A** on last 2 lps.

Row 3: Continuing with Colour **A**, Tss 3, work a LTfpdc in next st (1), *Tss 3 (2), work a LTfpdc in next st. Repeat from * to last st, replacing last LTfpdc with an end st. Return, changing back to Colour **B** on last 2 lps.

Row 4: Continuing with Colour **B**, work Tss to last st, work end st. Return, changing back to Colour **A** on last 2 lps.

Row 5: Continuing with Colour **A**, Tss 1, work a LTfpdc in next st, *Tss 3, work a LTfpdc in next st. Repeat from * to last 2 sts, Tss 1, work end st. Return, changing back to Colour **B** on last 2 lps.

Repeat Rows 2 – 5 for desired length.

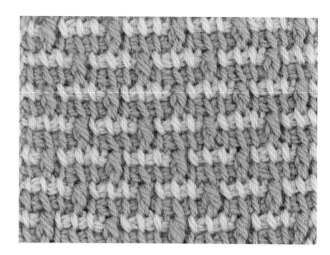

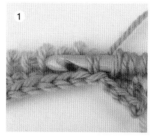

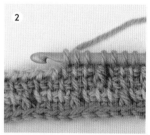

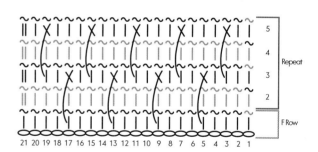

WAVE STITCH

- Multiples of 10+ 2
- 4 row pattern repeat
- First and last stitches do not form part of pattern and are always worked the same

Special Stitches and Techniques Used

Tunisian Simple Stitch (Tss): see Basic Stitches

Tunisian Double Crochet (Tdc): see Basic Stitches

Tunisian Slip Stitch (Tsl): pick up next vertical bar as if to Tss and leave it on hook without working the stitch

The following instructions are for a multicoloured wave. For a 2-colour wave, use Colour **B** for all Rows 2 and 4 of the repeat.

Row 1 (foundation row): Using Colour **A**, chain required number of stitches. Pick up a loop from back bump in 2nd ch from hook, and in each ch to end, leaving all loops on hook. Return, changing to Colour **B** on last 2 lps.

Row 2: Continuing with Colour **B**, *Tss 2, Tdc 4, Tss 2, Tsl 2 (1). Repeat from * to last st, work end st. Return, changing back to Colour **A** on last 2 lps.

Row 3: Continuing with Colour **A**, Tss to last st, work end st. Return, changing to Colour **C** on last 2 lps.

Row 4: Continuing with Colour **C**, ch1, Tdc in next st, *Tss 2, Tsl 2, Tss 2, Tdc 4 (2). Repeat from * to end, working last Tdc as end st. Return, changing back to Colour **A** on last 2 lps.

Row 5: Continuing with Colour **A**, Tss to end. Return, changing to next contrast colour on last 2 lps.

Repeat Rows 2-5 for desired length.

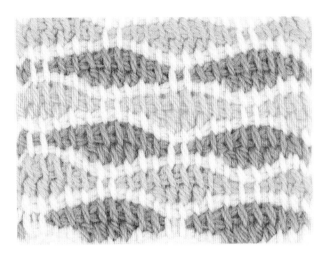

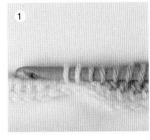
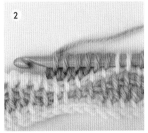

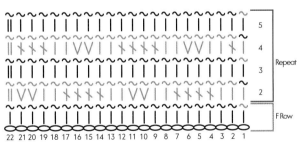

ARROWHEAD STITCH

- Multiples of 2
- 2 row pattern repeat
- First and last stitches do not form part of pattern and are always worked the same

Special Stitches and Techniques Used

Tunisian Simple Stitch (Tss): see Basic Stitches

Tunisian Full Stitch (Tfs): see Basic Stitches

Tss2tog: Insert hook under next 2 vertical bars, yo, pull up loop (1 lp on hook)

Row 1 (foundation row): Chain required number of stitches. Pick up a loop from back bump in 2nd ch from hook, and in each ch to end, leaving all loops on hook. Return.

Row 2: *Tss2tog (1), yo. Repeat from * to last st, work end stitch. Return.

Row 3: *Tss 1, Tfs in next sp (2). Repeat from * to last st, work end st. Return.

Repeat Rows 2-3 for desired length.

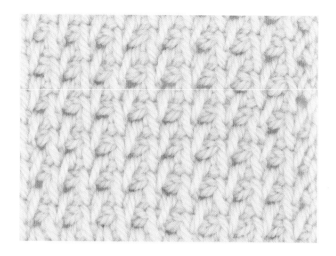

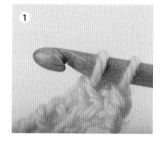

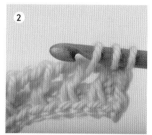

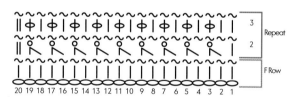

DIAGONAL EYELET

• Multiples of 4 + 1

• 4 row pattern repeat

• First and last stitches do not form part of pattern and are always worked the same

Special Stitches and Techniques Used

Tunisian Simple Stitch (Tss): see Basic Stitches

Tunisian Full Stitch (Tfs): see Basic Stitches

Special Tss (STss): insert hook under vertical bar and under adjacent top horizontal bar (1)

Row 1 (foundation row): Chain required number of stitches. Pick up a loop from back bump in 2nd ch from hook, and in each ch to end, leaving all loops on hook. Return.

Row 2: Tss 1, *yo, skip next st, STss 1, Tss 2. Repeat from * to last 3 sts, yo, skip next st, Tss 1, work end st. Return.

Row 3: *yo, skip next st, Tfs into sp (2), Tss 2. Repeat from * to to last 4 sts, yo, skip next st, Tfs 1, Tss 1 work end st. Return.

Row 4: Tfs 1, Tss 2, *yo, skip next st, Tfs into sp, Tss 2. Repeat from * to last st, work end st. Return.

Row 5: Tss 2, *yo, skip next st, Tfs into sp, Tss 2. Repeat from * to last 2 sts, yo, skip next st, work end st. Return.

Row 6: Tss 1, *yo, skip next st, Tfs into sp, Tss 2. Repeat from * to last 3 sts, yo, skip next st, Tfs 1, work end st. Return.

Repeat Rows 3-6 for desired length.

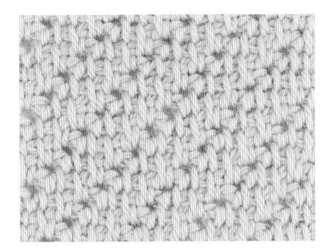

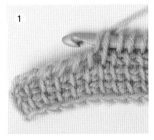

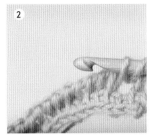

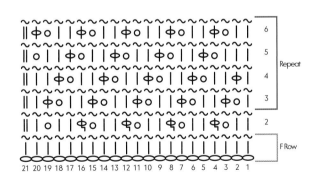

STAR STITCH

- Multiples of 9 + 2 + 2 (first and last sts)
- 4 row pattern repeat
- First and last stitches do not form part of pattern and are always worked the same

Special Stitches and Techniques Used

Tunisian Simple Stitch (Tss): see Basic Stitches

Tss5tog: insert hook under next 5 vertical bars, yo, draw up loop (1 lp on hook)

Row 1 (foundation row): Chain required number of stitches. Pick up a loop from back bump in 2nd ch from hook, and in each ch to end, leaving all loops on hook. Return.

Rows 2-3: Tss to last st, work end st. Return.

Row 4: Tss 3, *Tss5tog, (1) [yo, insert hook back through same sts, yo pull up loop] (2) twice more (5 lps back on hook) (3), Tss 4. Repeat from * to last st, work end st. Return.

Row 5: Note – take care not to miss the 2nd and 4th bars in star. These will be sitting back from from the rest of the sts (4). Tss to last st, work end st. Return.

Rows 6-7: Tss to last st, work end st. Return.

Repeat Rows 2-7 for desired length. You can also offset stars in alternative repeats by altering the number of Tss at the start of the row.

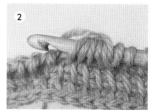
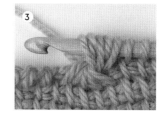

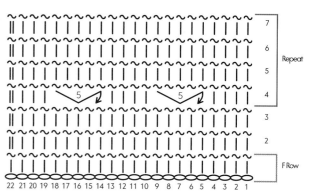

SCALLOP LACE

- Multiples of 5 + 2 (first and last sts)
- 2 row pattern repeat
- Pattern is formed by using a different return pass than normal in one of the pattern rows
- First and last stitches do not form part of pattern and are always worked the same

Stitches Used

Tunisian Simple Stitch (Tss): see Basic Stitches

Row 1 (foundation row): Chain required number of stitches. Pick up a loop from back bump in 2nd ch from hook, and in each ch to end, leaving all loops on hook. Return.

Row 2: Tss to last st, work end st. Return – yo, draw through 1 lp, ch 2 (1), *yo, draw through 6 lps (2), ch 4 (3). Repeat from * to last 2 lps on hook, ch 2, yo, draw through 2 lps.

Row 3: Tss into each st and into top of each cluster. Return with a regular return pass.

Repeat Rows 2-3 for desired length.

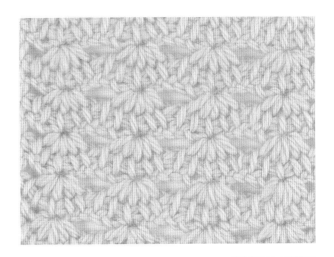

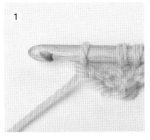

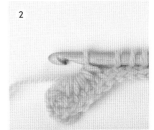

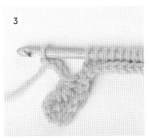

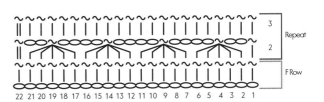

SHAPING

INCREASING

There are many different methods of increasing stitches in Tunisian crochet. There is no right or wrong way and each has its own characteristics, making it more or less suitable for a particular project. Some of the most common methods are shown here.

YARN OVER (YO)

• Suitable for use at the start, end or middle of a row

• Leaves a distinct hole in work

• Can be used as a decorative design feature

• Undesirable if you want an invisible increase

Before working the next stitch, yarn over hook, make next stitch as usual.

Return as normal.

M1 – BACK BUMP (M1BB)

• Suitable for use at the start, end or middle of a row

• Best method to use for an almost invisible finish

• It can be a little fiddly to pick up from the back bump
Insert hook into the bump behind the vertical bar of the next stitch.

Yo and draw up a loop (increase made).

Make next stitch according to pattern starting from the same vertical bar you just increased behind.

Return as normal.

M1 – TOP BAR (M1TB)

• Suitable for use at the start, end or middle of a row

• Leaves a small hole in work

• Can be used as a decorative design feature

• Undesirable if you want an invisible increase

Insert hook under the top bar of the horizontal bars sitting before next stitch.

Yo and draw up a loop (increase made).

Return as normal.

M1 – FULL STITCH (M1TFS)

• Suitable for use at the start, end or middle of a row

• Leaves a medium sized hole in work

• Can be used as a decorative design feature

• Undesirable if you want an invisible increase

Insert hook between two stitches.

Yo and draw up a loop (increase made).

Return as normal.

ADD MULTIPLE STITCHES – START OF ROW

• Only suitable to use when a multiple number of stitches are required at the start of a row

• Any number of stitches can be added

Before beginning the forward pass on the row you wish to increase, chain the required number of extra stitches.

Starting from the 2nd chain from hook, pick up a loop from each chain.

Once you reach the end of the chain, continue working in pattern from the original piece, starting from the first edge stitch that was previously unworked but has now combined with the increased stitches. Return as normal.

NOTE

THIS TYPE OF INCREASE IS USED WHEN A DRAMATIC CHANGE IN SHAPE IS REQUIRED. FOR EXAMPLE, ADDING SLEEVES TO AN ALL-IN-ONE GARMENT OR CONSTRUCTING A SHAPED PICTURE MOTIF.

ADD MULTIPLE STITCHES – END OF ROW

• Only suitable to use when a multiple number of stitches are required at the end of a row

• Any number of stitches can be added

At the end of the forward pass on the row you wish to increase, use a separate piece of yarn to make a chain with the required number of extra stitches. Attach chain length to end of hook. The first st of this new ch becomes a st. Starting from 2nd ch from hook, continue picking up loops from chain. Return as normal.

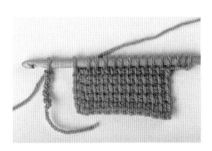

DECREASING

There are several options for decreasing stitches in Tunisian crochet and all are very easy to do. Some are more suitable than others depending where they will be placed in a row.

SKIP ONE (SK1)

• Best used within the body of a row. Can be used at the start or end of a row but can have a messy appearance

• Leaves a small hole if made on the very edge of work

Skip over the next stitch without working and continue working on from the next stitch.

Return as normal.

WORK 2 TOGETHER

• Will be abbreviated depending on stitch type eg. Tss2tog, Tks2tog

• Best used within the body of a row. Can be used at the start or end of a row but can have a messy appearance

• Leaves a small hole if made on the very edge of the work

Insert hook through the next two stitches at the same time according to the stitch type you are making i.e. if you are working in Tss then you would slide your hook under the next 2 bars.

Yarn over and pull through both loops leaving one loop on hook.

Return as normal.

RETURN PASS DECREASE

- Best used at the start and end of a row

- Can be used in the middle of a row but not recommended

- This type of decrease is used in Tunisian Entrelac crochet

Depending on the pattern and where the decrease is required, you will be asked to 'yarn over and pull through X number of loops' on the return pass.

If the decrease is at the start of the return pass (decrease on left edge) then you will pull through 2 loops instead of the usual 1 loop.

If the decrease is at the end of the return pass (decrease on right edge) then you will pull through the last 3 loops instead of the usual 2 loops.

If the decrease is in the middle of the row, then you will pull through 3 loops instead of the usual 2 loops.

The instructions below are for decreasing at either end of a row.

Work forward pass as normal. Begin the return pass with yarn over and pull through 2 loops (decrease made), continue pulling through 2 loops until you reach the last 3 loops on your hook, pull through 3 loops (decrease made).

When working the next forward pass of a row after making a decrease, the bar of the stitch just decreased will still be visible but will not be worked.

At the start of a forward pass, skip the 2nd vertical bar.

At the end of a forward pass, skip the 2nd last vertical bar.

MULTIPLE STITCH DECREASE

- Used when a dramatic change in shape is required, for example when shaping armholes in a garment
At the start of a row, bind off the required number of stitches. Work remaining stitches as normal up to the point where you need to decrease stitches at the end of the row.

Bind off the required number of stitches. Break off the yarn and rejoin to remaining live stitches. Return as normal. Continue working on remaining stitches for desired length.

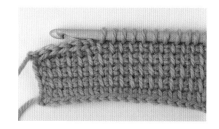

SHORT ROWS

Short rows are a great way to create shaping or a design feature in your work. Depending how they are made, they can create gentle curves for items such as shawls, add ease to garments for areas such as the bust or even create a sock heel or a circular piece.

To explain short rows simply, you basically work only a partial row before returning and continuing on to work subsequent rows.

The number of stitches and rows in a short row section will vary depending on the desired function or shape.

The following instructions will show you how to work a partial row and how to treat the last stitch of your short rows. If you'd like to practice making short rows, try out the circular base of the Entrelac Bag (see Entrelac Bag).

STEP 1

Forward: Work the required number of stitches to complete a partial row (1). Photo shows short row loops in contrast colour.

Return: As normal.

STEP 2

Forward: On the following full length row after a short row, pick up all the loops from the short row as normal. When you reach the end of the short row, continue picking up loops from the previous full length row to the last st, work end st (2).

Return: As normal.

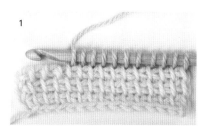

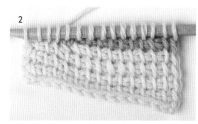

JOINING

JOIN-AS-YOU-GO

Joining as you go is used when working a piece in strips. You will begin by completing the first strip before joining subsequent strips as you go. This method has a seamless, almost invisible appearance.

The photos below show the front (top) and back (bottom) of two strips that have been joined using the join-as-you-go method.

COMPLETE YOUR FIRST STRIP

To start a new strip, join yarn in the lower right corner of the previous strip with a slip stitch. Chain the required number of stitches loosely for the next strip.

Foundation row: Draw up a loop from each chain across as usual for a foundation row.

When you reach the previous strip, insert your hook into the "V" of the edge stitch and through the loop directly behind it at the back of your work. Return: Yarn over and draw through these loops and the next loop on your hook (this will be the last loop of the foundation row just made), yarn over and draw through two loops to the end of the row as usual.

Subsequent rows: Work all stitches on your forward pass as usual, join as described above when you reach the end of the row. Return as you did in the foundation row.

CROCHET TOGETHER

These photos show the front (top) and back (bottom) of two strips that have been crocheted together.

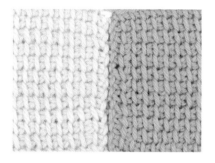

SEW TOGETHER WITH MATTRESS STITCH

Hold pieces to be joined with right sides together. Attach yarn with a slip knot to a regular crochet hook of the same size used for your Tunisian piece.

Insert hook under the edge stitches of both pieces, yo and pull through both loops on hook (slip stitch made). Continue along edge.

The photos below show the front (top) and back (bottom) of two strips that have been sewn together with mattress stitch.

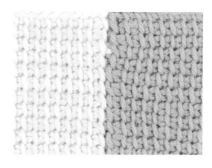

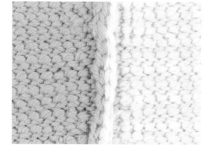

Lay out pieces side by side with right sides facing up.

Insert needle through the corner of one piece leaving a long tail end.

Insert needle through the corner of the other piece, then through both pieces again to secure.

Insert needle under the horizontal bars next to the edge stitch on one of the pieces. Repeat on the other piece, working into the bars next to the corresponding edge stitch.

Continue making pairs of stitches this way, pulling up the thread every few stitches or so. Pull the thread fairly firmly so that the stitches disappear into the seam, being careful not to pull too tightly and distort the fabric.

NOTE

YOU CAN ALSO JOIN PIECES USING SINGLE CROCHET INSTEAD OF A SLIP STITCH, AND YOU CAN USE IT AS A DESIGN FEATURE. IF YOU HOLD THE PIECES WRONG SIDES TOGETHER, THE JOIN WILL SHOW ON THE RIGHT SIDE OF YOUR WORK AS A RAISED DESIGN.

WORKING IN THE ROUND

Working Tunisian crochet in the round is a great way to create seamless projects such as hats, baskets, gloves or socks.

There are some differences between working in the round and working flat. Tunisian crochet in the round is worked with just a few stitches at a time and in spiral rounds, using a double-ended hook and two separate balls of yarn for each of the forward and return passes.

Often seen worked with two contrasting colours, it is also possible to use the same coloured yarn for each pass such as in the Ribbed Cowl (see Ribbed Cowl) or a bit of both as in the Tassel Pouch (see Tassel Pouch).

FOUNDATION ROUND

Step 1: Chain required number of stitches with Yarn **A**. Join with a sl st to first chain being careful not to twist your chain (1).

Step 2: Insert hook into the back bump of next ch, *yo and pull up a loop. Place a marker in this first stitch and continue picking up loops this way until you have picked up as many stitches that will comfortably fit on your hook (2).

Step 3: Flip your hook, and slide the stitches to the other end of hook. Yarn **A** will now be sitting to the right at the end of your stitches (3).

Step 4: Using Yarn **B**, yo and pull through the first loop (4). *Yo and pull through 2 loops. Repeat from * until you have 3 loops left on your hook (5).

Step 5: Flip the hook and slide stitches back to the other end.

Repeat Steps 2-5 until you reach the end of the chain (foundation row made).

ROUNDS

You will now begin working in spiral rounds moving your marker up on the first stitch as you go (6).

Step 6: Insert hook under first marked st, yo and pull up loop. Continue pulling up loops until you have picked up as many stitches as will comfortably fit.

Step 7: Flip your hook (7) and slide stitches to the other end of hook.

Step 8: *Yo and pull through 2 loops. Repeat from * until you have 3 loops left on your hook.

Repeat Steps 6-8 until you reach the desired length.

Bind off (see Basic Stitches).

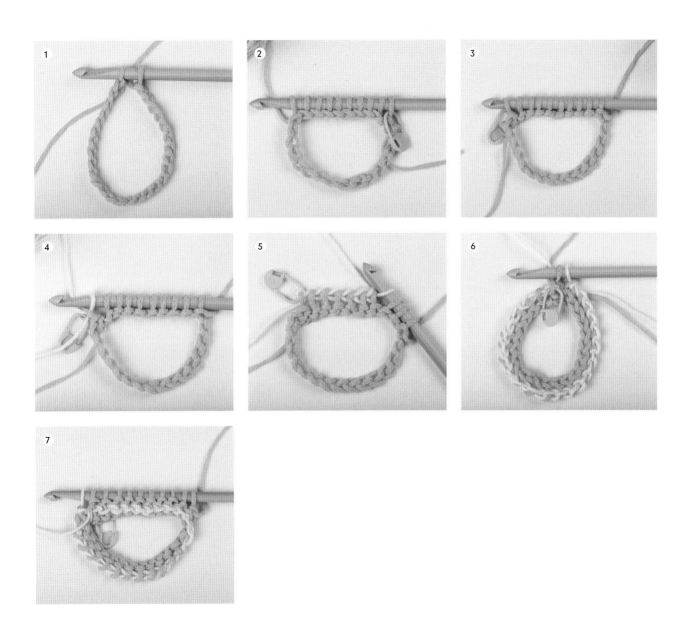

FINISHING

WEAVE ENDS IN

Don't be tempted to just snip off your yarn ends! It's a necessary evil if you don't want all your hard work to fall apart.

Thread a tapestry needle with the yarn end and weave it in through the back bumps of stitches. Start in a downwards direction for a few stiches, move over by a stitch and work the end back in an upwards direction. If you still have a bit of yarn left, work back down once more.

Pull yarn end up slightly before snipping off.

BLOCKING

Blocking is your best friend in Tunisian crochet! It's not anyone's favourite thing to do after completing a project, but it really does make all the difference in taming that curl. Not only will it straighten out your work, it will also settle your stitches and enhance the drape of the fabric.

To give you an example of the dramatic difference that blocking can make, the photos to the right show a before and after picture of a swatch of Tunisian Simple Stitch made in 100% wool, blocked using the wet block method. Notice how the curl has disappeared and the yarn has bloomed, settling the stitches. The yarn also has an enhanced drape and feels softer to the touch.

There are several methods of blocking that can be used and some are more suitable than others depending on your yarn and type of project. Natural fibres tend to react better to blocking than acrylic. It is still possible to block acrylic yarns but as they are all different in composition the results can be unpredictable.

If you are using acrylic yarn it is best to stick with the wet or spray blocking methods. If you wish to use the steam method, do so on the cautious side and do a swatch test first to avoid melting the fibres and ruining all your hard work (see instructions for more detail).

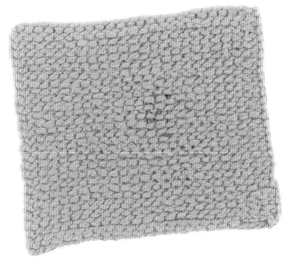

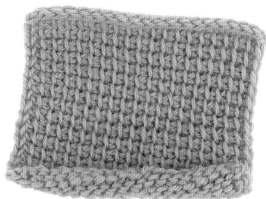

Before blocking

After blocking

I personally prefer the wet block method for most of my projects, especially blankets as it also gives me the opportunity to wash them at the same time, but I encourage you to try out each method for yourself on a small swatch and notice the difference it makes to your work.

What you'll need:

• A basin or tub large enough to hold your project.

• Blocking board – this can be any flat surface such as foam board, mattress or carpeted floor. For items that are not flat, such as hats, a blown up balloon or scrunched up plastic bags will work. Place them inside the item so that it holds its shape as it dries.

• Rust proof pins.

• Several towels to use for laying under your work and removing excess water.

WET BLOCK

Lay a towel (or towels, depending on the size of your project) over a flat surface such as a foam blocking board, mattress or floor.

Fill a basin large enough to hold your project with tepid water. Lay out another towel next to your work area to assist with removing excess water later.

Submerge your work in water and let it soak for a couple of minutes to ensure it is completely saturated.

Let the water out of the basin and gently squeeze out water, being careful not to rub, wring or twist your work.

Place item onto towel and roll up tightly to remove excess water.

Spread item out onto blocking board, smoothing it out with your hand and straightening edges as you go.

Place pins in corners and along edges to hold in place, being careful not to distort the shape of your item.

Leave to dry.

SPRAY BLOCK

Pin item into shape on a blocking board.

Spray item with cold water using a spray bottle until completely wet, press down with your hand as you work.

Leave to dry.

STEAM BLOCK

Safety note: Steam burns and pins get red hot! Keep your hands well away from underneath the iron as you are steaming and don't be tempted to adjust your work as you go. If you do need to make any adjustments, put the iron down first and wait until the pins and your item have cooled down before touching.

Acrylic yarn: It is important to do a swatch test on acrylic yarn first as it will melt at a certain heat point. All acrylic yarns are different so how much heat a yarn can tolerate will vary. Start out holding the iron about 15cm (6in) away from the work and gradually move in closer (but never closer than 3cm (1⅛in) above work). Stop when you notice your work is straightening out without the yarn being affected.

• Pin item into shape on a blocking board.

• Using an iron set on the highest steam setting, hold iron about 2cm above the item (or more if you are using acrylic yarn – see safety note).

• Move the iron slowly over the item allowing the steam to penetrate for a couple of seconds before moving to the next section.

• Leave to completely cool and dry.

CROCHET BORDER

Not only will adding a crochet border finish your work off nicely it will also help to straighten out any curl.

You can use any crochet border design you fancy and it can be added in a couple of ways:

• Simply work straight into each stitch around the edge of your work and begin crocheting your border as per your chosen pattern.

• Sometimes working stitches directly into your Tunisian crochet can result in small holes showing, especially along the sides of your work. To avoid these unsightly holes, first work a row of slip stitches around your piece in the same colour that will be used for the border.
Begin your crochet border by working your hook under these slip stitches. This method produces a very neat finish.

EMBELLISHMENT

The fabric created with Tunisian crochet makes a fantastic backdrop for embellishment. Add individual touches to your work with any or all of these techniques. Let your imagination soar! Here are just a few ideas to get you started.

Make a small stitch at the back of the work to secure your thread and leave a long tail to weave in later.

Starting at the base of a stitch, bring your needle out on the inside of the vertical bar (point 1) and take it across to the outside top of the next bar (point 2). Continue working diagonally this way for the required number of stitches.

Complete the cross by returning in the opposite direction.

CROSS STITCH

The grid like pattern created with Tunisian Simple stitch lends itself beautifully to cross stitch. Any cross stitch graph can be used to embellish your Tunisian crochet work.

DUPLICATE STITCH

Another way to add graphic designs to your work is Duplicate stitch. As the name suggests, it looks just like stockinette stitch, or in Tunisian crochet terms, Tunisian Knit stitch. This method can only be done on a Knit stitch piece, but it is a good alternative if you prefer not to get tangled in yarn by working stranded colour work or intarsia.

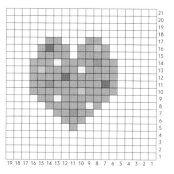

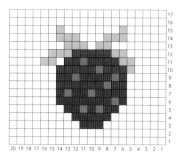

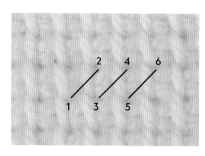

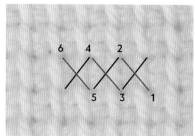

Thread a tapestry needle with yarn that is the same or thicker than that used in the piece to be worked on.

Make a small stitch at the back of the work to secure and leave a long tail to weave in later.

Bring your needle from the back to the front at the base of the stitch to be duplicated (point 1)

Insert your needle from right (point 2) to left (point 3) behind both sides of the stitch above.

Complete the stitch by inserting the needle front to back at the base of the stitch (point 4).

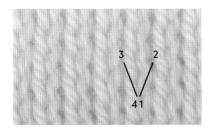

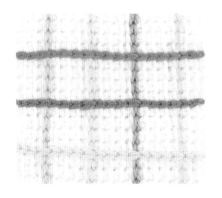

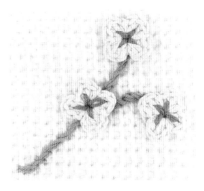

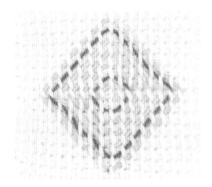

WEAVING

There are no limits when it comes to weaving on Tunisian crochet. Thread any interesting fibre or novelty yarn through the stitches to create an individual piece.

You can weave on almost any stitch type and in any direction. Here, I have woven yarn diagonally to form a pattern on Tunisian Simple stitch.

SURFACE CHAIN

Whether it be straight lines or spirals, surface chain is an easy way to add another dimension to your work. Stitches are formed with a slip stitch and are worked from the front to the back of the work.

With a slip knot on your hook, make a slip stitch near your starting point at the back of your work.

Remove hook and insert it from the front of the work in the same place. Grab the loop from the back of the work and pull through to the front. You will now have a loop at the front of your work and the working tail of yarn at the back.

Insert your hook in the next stitch from front to back, grab the yarn from the back and pull through to the front to complete the stitch.

EMBROIDERY AND 3D CROCHET ELEMENTS

If you are an embroiderer, you can use any embroidery stitch to add interest to your work. Or why not attach some crochet flowers to make a wonderful 3-dimensional piece?

In the sample shown, I have embroidered a branch with Stem Stitch and sewn on some tiny crocheted cherry blossom flowers.

THE PROJECTS

Now that you've practiced your stitches and worked some swatches it's finally time to make something!

All of the following projects use stitches explained in the book and are a great way to improve your Tunisian crochet skills, while making some lovely items for yourself and your home.

TASSEL POUCH

Worked in the round with a colour-block design of
Honeycomb Stitch and Simple Stitch, these handy
little pouches are perfect for gift giving or for
keeping your bits and bobs organised.

HOOK

5mm (US H8) double-ended
Tunisian hook

YARN

Aran weight (10-ply) cotton yarn in
the following colours:

A Contrast Colour – 50g

B Main Colour – 50g

NOTE

DIVIDE BALL B IN HALF. THE FIRST
HALF WILL BE USED FOR THE RETURN
PASS OF THE 2-TONE CONTRAST
SECTION AND WILL BE REFERRED TO
AS YARN B1. WE'LL CALL THE OTHER
HALF YARN B2, WHICH WILL BE
USED FOR THE FORWARD PASS OF
THE SOLID COLOUR SECTION.

OTHER MATERIALS

18cm (7in) zip

Lining fabric

Sewing needle and thread to match
main pouch colour

Embroidery floss – 1 skein each of 2
different colours for tassel

1 x 10mm (³/₈in) jump ring (used for
jewellery making)

Sewing machine (optional)

SPECIAL STITCHES AND
TECHNIQUES USED

Tunisian Simple Stitch (Tss): see
Basic Stitches

Tunisian Purl Stitch (Tps): see Basic
Stitches

Working in the Round: see Working
in the Round

FINISHED SIZE

18 x 12cm (7 x 5in)

POUCH CHART

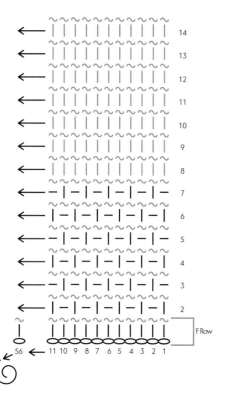

POUCH

Foundation Row: Using Yarn **A** ch 56. Being careful not to twist ch, join with a sl st into first ch to form a circle. Pick up a loop from back bump in next ch and place marker in first st. *Continue picking up stitches this way until you have filled about half of your hook, flip hook and begin the return pass for these stitches using Yarn **B1**. Repeat from * until you reach marker in first st.

NOTE

THE FOLLOWING ROUNDS ARE WORKED IN A SPIRAL. MOVE THE MARKER UP ON THE FIRST STITCH AS YOU WORK EACH ROUND.

Round 2: With Yarn **A**, *Tss 1, Tps 1. Repeat from * until you have enough sts on your hook, flip work and return with Yarn **B1** until you have 3 sts on hook. Repeat from * to end.

Round 3: With Yarn **A**, *Tps 1, Tss 1. Repeat from * until you have enough sts on your hook, flip work and return with Yarn **B1** until you have 3 sts on hook. Repeat from * to end.

Round 4: Work as for Round 2.

Round 5: Work as for Round 3.

Round 6: Work as for Round 2.

Round 7: Work as for Round 3 up to last st. On the return for the last set of stitches, return through all Yarn **A** stitches, leaving 1st of Yarn **B1** on hook. Cut Yarn **A** and tie off.

Round 8: Join Yarn **B2** with a yarn over on next st. (You will now have two loops of the same colour on your hook. **B2** is used for the Forward pass and **B1** is used for the Return Pass). *Tss in each st until you have enough sts on your hook, flip work and return with Yarn **B1** until you have 3 sts on hook. Repeat from * to end.

Rounds 9-14: Using Yarn **B2**, *Tss in each st until you have enough sts on your hook, flip work and return with Yarn **B1** until you have 3 sts on hook. Repeat from * to end.

Bind off and weave in ends.

TASSEL POUCH

FINISHING

Hand stitch zip into place along top edge of pouch. Don't worry too much about neatness as your stitches will be covered with the lining on the inside and will disappear amongst the crochet stitches on the outside.

LINING

Cut a rectangle of lining fabric measuring 20 x 25cm (8 x 10in).

Fold fabric in half with right sides together.

Stitch along both sides with a 2cm (³/₄in) seam allowance.

Fold back a 2cm (³/₄in) hem around the top edge.

Place lining inside pouch and hand stitch lining to zipper tape using an invisible stitch (see Techniques).

TASSEL

Decide your main tassel colour and take bands off this skein.

Cut 2 x 90cm (35¹/₂in) lengths from the other skein.

Tie the end of one of the lengths of contrast colour around the main colour skein, 5cm (2in) from one end. Wind this colour around the skein for 5cm, working over the tail end as you go. To finish, thread the end onto a tapestry needle and work the needle back down through the wrapped yarn as far as you can go before cutting off as close as possible.

Fold the tassel in half, and using the other length of contrast colour start winding around the base of the wrapped yarn covering the end as you go. Finish off the tail end as you did in the previous step.

Trim the tassel ends evenly.

Open up the jump ring with your fingers and pierce it through the top of the tassel. Attach it to the zipper pull and close the ring.

ENTRELAC BAG

With its short strap and wide opening, this Tunisian entrelac bag also converts into a basket. This makes it perfect for keeping your latest project in, ready to pick up and take along with you to your next crafternoon or car trip.

HOOK

5mm (US H8) regular crochet hook (without a handle)

5mm Tunisian hook

YARN

DK (8-ply) cotton yarn in the following colours – used double throughout:

A Denim Blue – 50g

B Turquoise – 100g

C Pink – 50g

D Lime – 50g

E Purple – 50g

F Light Blue – 100g

G Coral – 50g

H Yellow – 50g

I Hot Pink – 50g

J Jade – 50g

SPECIAL STITCHES AND TECHNIQUES USED

Tunisian Simple Stitch (Tss): see Basic Stitches

Short Rows: see Shaping

Single crochet (sc): see Techniques

Half double crochet (hdc): see Techniques

Crab stitch: see Techniques

Regular single crochet in back of loop (Sc blo): insert hook under the back loop only of the next stitch, yo and complete sc as normal

Make one (M1): insert hook into space before next vertical bar (as in Tunisian full stitch), yo and pull up a loop.

FINISHED SIZE

20 x 27cm (7⁷⁄₈ x 10⁵⁄₈in)

NOTE

YARN IS USED DOUBLE THROUGHOUT THIS PATTERN.

BASE

NOTE

Step 1: Using Colour **A** and regular crochet hook, make a magic ring.

Step 2: Make 6 sc into ring. Join with a ss to first st. Don't fasten off.

Step 3: Switch to Tunisian hook and ch 14. Starting in second ch from hook and keeping all loops on hook, pick up a lp in each of the next 13 ch and 1 lp from same sc as start of ch (15 lps on hook). **Return:** yo, pull through 2 lps to end. The return for these joining rows is different to the return on the following short rows.

WEDGE 1

Step 4: Tss 2 (3 lps on hook). Return.

Step 5: Tss 4 (5 lps on hook). Return.

Step 6: Tss 6 (7 lps on hook). Return.

Step 7: Tss 8 (9 lps on hook). Return.

Step 8: Tss 10 (11 lps on hook). Return.

Step 9: Tss 12 (13 lps on hook). Return, changing to Colour **B** on last st.

Step 10: (first row of next wedge) Continuing in Colour **B**, Tss 12, insert

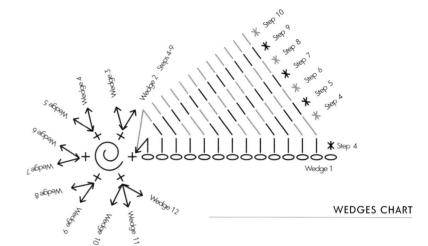

WEDGES CHART

hook into same sc as start of wedge and pull up a lp (14 lps on hook). **Return:** yo, pull through 2 lps to end.

WEDGE 2

Steps 4-9: Work as for Wedge 1, changing to Colour **A** on last st of step 9.

Step 10: work as for Wedge 1, inserting hook into **next** sc at end of row, pull up a lp (14 lps on hook). **Return:** yo, pull through 2 lps to end.

WEDGE 3

Steps 4-9: Work as for Wedge 1.

Step 10: work as for Wedge 1, inserting hook into **same** sc, pull up a lp (14 lps on hook). **Return:** yo, pull through 2 lps to end.

WEDGES 4, 6, 8 AND 10

Work as for Wedge 2.

WEDGES 5, 7, 9 AND 11

Work as for Wedge 3.

WEDGE 12

Steps 4-8: Work as for Wedge 1.

Step 9: Tss 12, insert hook into **next** sc at end of row, pull up a lp (14 lps on hook). **Return:** yo, pull through 2 lps to end. Fasten off, leaving long tail for joining.

Join Wedge 12 to Wedge 1 using ladder stitch (see Techniques), working under horizontal bars. (84 sts)

SIDES

NOTE

THE FIRST TWO ROUNDS ARE WORKED IN REGULAR CROCHET. A REGULAR CROCHET HOOK CAN BE USED FOR THE TUNISIAN ENTRELAC ROUNDS AS YOU WILL ONLY HAVE A FEW STITCHES ON YOUR HOOK AT A TIME.

Round 1: Join Colour **B** with a ss into any colour join between two wedges, *sc 3, 2 sc into next st. Repeat from * to end. Join with a ss into first sc, working into the back loop only (sc blo). (105 sc)

Round 2: Ch 1 (not counted as st), sc blo in same st, sc blo into each st to end. Join with ss into first sc.

ROUND 3 (BASE TRIANGLES)

Row 1: Continuing with Colour **B**, pull up a lp in next st (2 lps on hook). Return.

Row 2: M1, Tss in next vertical bar, pull up lp in next sc (4 lps on hook). Return.

Row 3: Tss in next 2 vertical bars, M1 between last st worked and end st, pull up lp in next sc (5 lps on hook). Return.

Row 4: Tss in next 3 vertical bars, M1 between last st worked and end st, pull up lp in next sc (6 lps on hook). Return.

Row 5: Tss in next 4 vertical bars, M1 between last st worked and end st, pull up lp in next sc (7 lps on hook). Return.

Row 6: Tss in next 5 vertical bars, M1 between last st worked and end st, pull up lp in next sc (8 lps on hook). Return.

Row 7: Bind off 6 sts, ss into same sp as last st in last row (first triangle complete).

Repeat Rows 1-7 fourteen more times (15 triangles). Fasten off.

ROUND 4 (BEGINNING OF ENTRELAC SQUARES)

Square One

Row 1: Join Colour **C** with a ss into the top right hand corner of any triangle (this will be the first st of the last row of the triangle), pick up a lp in each of the next 5 sts (along bind off edge of triangle), pick up a lp from first st on the side of the next triangle (7 lps on hook). **Return:** yo and pull through 2 lps to end.

Rows 2-5: Tss in next 5 sts, pick up a lp from side of the next triangle (7 lps on hook). **Return:** yo and pull through 2 lps to end.

Bind off. Ss back into same sp as last st. Repeat Square One to end of round

Round 5:

Square One

Row 1: Join Colour **D** with a ss into the top right hand corner of any square, pick up a lp in each of the next 5 sts and 1 lp from the side of the next square (7 lps on hook). **Return:** yo and pull through 2 lps to end.

Rows 2-5: Tss in next 5 sts, pick up a lp from side of the next square (7 lps on hook). **Return:** yo and pull through 2 lps to end.

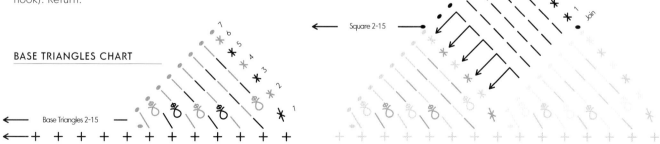

BASE TRIANGLES CHART

Base Triangles 2-15

ENTRELAC SQUARES CHART

Square 2-15

Join

EYELET SQUARE CHART

Bind off, ss back into same sp as last st.

Repeat Square One to end of round.

Round 6: Join Colour **E**, work as for Round 5.

Round 7: Join Colour **F**, work as for Round 5.

Round 8: Join Colour **G**, work as for Round 5.

Round 9: Join Colour **H**, work as for Round 5.

Round 10: Join Colour **I**, work as for Round 5.

Round 11: Join Colour **J**, work as for Round 5.

Round 12 (eyelet round): You will now work a row of eyelet squares as follows, making eyelets in every second square. Every other square to be worked as per previous pattern.

NOTE

YOU WILL FINISH THE ROUND WITH 2 EYELET SQUARES NEXT TO EACH OTHER AT THE FRONT OF THE BAG (8 EYELET SQUARES AND 7 PLAIN SQUARES).

Eyelet Square

Row 1: Join Colour **B** with a ss into the top right hand corner of **third** square, pick up a lp in each of the next 5 sts and 1 lp from the side of the next square (7 lps on hook). **Return:** yo and pull through 2 lps to end.

Row 2: Tss in next 5 sts, pick up a lp from side of the next square (7 lps on hook). **Return:** yo and pull through 2 lps to end.

Row 3: Tss in next 2 sts, yo, sk next st, Tss in next 2 sts, pick up a lp from side of next square (7 lps on hook). **Return:** yo and pull through 2 lps to end.

Row 4: Tss in next 2 sts, pick up lp from eyelet sp, Tss in next 2 sts, pick up a lp from side of next square (7 lps on hook). **Return:** yo and pull through 2 lps to end.

Row 5: Tss in next 5 sts, pick up a lp from side of next square (7 lps on hook). **Return:** yo and pull through 2 lps to end.

Bind off, ss back into same sp as last st.

Repeat this Eyelet Square on every **second** square, working every other square as per previous pattern to end of round.

ROUND 13 (STRAIGHT EDGE TRIANGLES)

Row 1: Join Colour **C** with a ss into the top right hand corner of any square, pick up a lp in each of the next 5 sts and 1 lp from the side of the next square (7 lps on hook). **Return:** yo and pull through 2 lps to last 3 lps on hook, yo and pull through 3 lps.

Row 2: Sk next vertical bar, Tss 4, pick up a lp from side of the next square (6 lps on hook). **Return:** yo and pull through 2 loops to last 3 lps on hook, yo and pull through 3 lps.

Row 3: Sk next vertical bar, Tss 3, pick up a lp from side of the next square (5 lps on hook). **Return:** yo and pull through 2 lps to last 3 lps on hook, yo and pull through 3 lps.

Row 4: Sk next vertical bar, Tss 2, pick up a lp from side of the next square (4 lps on hook). **Return:** yo and pull through 2 lps to last 3 lps on hook, yo and pull through 3 lps.

Row 5: Sk next vertical bar, Tss 1, pick up a lp from side of the next square (3 lps on hook). **Return:** yo and pull through 3 lps. Ss back into same sp on side of square.

Repeat Rows 1-5 to end of round. Don't fasten off at end of round.

NOTE

THE FOLLOWING ROUNDS ARE WORKED IN REGULAR CROCHET.

Round 14: Continuing with Colour **C**, hdc into each st to end. Join with a ss into first hdc. Fasten off.

Round 15: Join Colour **D** into first st, work in Crab st to end. Fasten off.

STRAP

Using Colour **F** and leaving a long tail for sewing onto bag later, ch 55.

Row 1: sc into second ch from hook, sc into each st to end (54sc).

Rows 2-5: Ch 1 (not counted as st) sc into same st and into each st to end. Turn.

Fasten off, leaving a long tail for sewing onto bag.

ICORD

Step 1: Using Colour **F**, ch 3.

Step 2: Pick up loop from second ch and keep on hook, repeat for next ch (3 lps on hook).

Step 3: Carefully remove first 2 lps on hook and hold onto with your free hand, ch 1 through remaining loop on hook.

Step 4: Place second lp back on your hook, ch 1.

Step 5: Place third lp back on your hook, ch 1.

Repeat Steps 3-5 until cord measures 85cm (33$\frac{1}{2}$in). Yo and pull through all 3 lps to bind off.

Thread tail ends onto a yarn needle and carefully go back up through the centre of the cord as far as you can. Pull up slightly and snip off, letting the end disappear back inside the cord.

FINISHING

Fold bag in half to find sides, place end of strap approximately 5cm (2in) down from the top on the inside of the bag and stitch strap into place. Repeat on other side.

Thread icord through eyelet and tie a knot in each end.

RIBBED COWL

This warm and cosy cowl is made in the round using a chunky yarn and 2 x 1 rib pattern which looks just like knitting. The simple, unfussy design makes it perfect for both men and women and it is sure to keep you warm on chilly days.

HOOK
7mm double-ended Tunisian hook

YARN
Aran weight (10-ply) yarn in the same colour:

A used for forward pass – 50g

B used for return pass – 50g

GAUGE
15 rows x 14 sts in rib pattern

SPECIAL STITCHES AND TECHNIQUES USED
Tunisian Knit Stitch (Tks): see Basic Stitches

Tunisian Purl Stitch (Tps): see Basic Stitches

Working in the Round: see Working in the Round

FINISHED SIZE
80 x 25cm (32 x 10in)

COWL

Foundation Row: Using Yarn **A**, ch 110. Being careful not to twist ch, join with a sl st into first ch to form a circle. Pick up a loop from back bump in next ch and place marker in first st. *Continue picking up stitches this way until you have filled about half of your hook, flip the hook and begin the return pass for these stitches using Yarn **B**. Repeat from * until you reach marker in first st.

NOTE

THE FOLLOWING ROUNDS ARE WORKED IN A SPIRAL. MOVE YOUR MARKER UP TO THE FIRST STITCH OF EACH ROUND AS YOU WORK.

Round 2: With Yarn **A** Tps1, *Tks 2, Tps 1. Flip work and return with Yarn **B** once you have enough sts on your hook. Repeat from * to end.

Continue working in spiral rounds as for Round 2 until your work measures 25cm (10in) or your preferred width.

Bind off and weave in ends.

COWL CHART

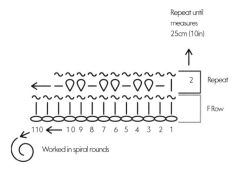

RIBBED COWL

SIMPLE SCARF

This easy scarf is worked on the principle of increasing until you have used up half your skein of yarn and then decreasing until the yarn is finished. It looks stunning in any type of yarn, whether it be a long striping gradient sock yarn as used in this model or a plain yarn. You could also use thicker yarn for a longer and wider scarf.

HOOK
5mm straight or cable hook

YARN
100g (400m/440yd) fingering weight yarn

GAUGE
5cm = 14 sts x 10 rows of Tss (before blocking)

SPECIAL STITCHES AND TECHNIQUES USED
Tunisian Simple Stitch (Tss): see Basic Stitches

Tunisian Full Stitch (Tfs): see Basic Stitches

Increase: see Techniques

Decrease: see Techniques

M1bb (Make 1 – back bump): pick up a loop from the back bump of the return chain behind the next vertical bar, Tss into same vertical bar (1 st increased)

Tss2tog: insert hook under next 2 vertical bars, yo, pull up loop (decrease made)

Special Tss (STss): insert hook under vertical bar **and** under adjacent top horizontal bar (this gives extra stability to Tss in eyelet rows)

FINISHED SIZE
210cm long x 20cm at widest point (83 x 8in) after blocking

SCARF CHART

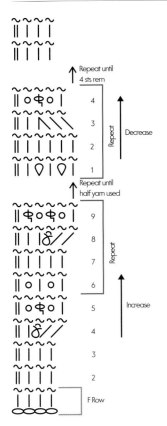

FIRST HALF (INCREASE)

Foundation Row: Ch 4. Pick up a loop from back bump in 2nd ch from hook, and in each ch to end, leaving all loops on hook. Return.

Row 2: Tss to last st, work end st. Return.

Row 3: Tss to last st, work end st. Return.

Row 4: Tss 1, M1bb, Tss to last st, work end st. Return (5 lps).

Row 5: *Yo, sk next st, STss into next st, yo, sk next st, work end st. Return.

Row 6: *Tfs into eyelet sp, Tss into next st. Repeat from * to last st, work end st. Return.

Plain rows with an odd number of sts will end with '1 Tfs, work end st'.

Plain rows with an even number of sts will end with '1 Tfs, 1 Tss, work end st'.

Row 7: Tss to last st, work end st. Return.

Row 8: Tss 1, M1bb, Tss to last st, work end st. Return.

Row 9: *Yo, sk next st, STss into next st. Repeat from * to last st. Return.

Eyelet rows with an odd number of sts will end with 'yo, sk next st, work end st'.

Eyelet rows with an even number of sts will end with 'yo, sk next st, STss, work end st'.

Repeat Rows 6 – 9 until half of your yarn has been used ending with Row 9.

SECOND HALF (DECREASE)

See increase half for instructions on end of rows.

Row 1: *Tfs into eyelet sp, Tss into next st. Repeat from * to last st. Return.

Row 2: Tss to last st, work end st. Return.

Row 3: Tss 1, Tss2tog, Tss to last st, work end st. Return.

Row 4: *Yo, sk next st, STss into next st. Repeat from * to last st. Return.

Repeat Rows 1-4 until you have 4 sts left on hook. Work another 2 rows of Tss. Bind off.

FINISHING

Block your scarf to open up the lacy eyelet pattern.

Add tassels or pompoms to the ends if desired.

HERRINGBONE CUSHION

Constructed in three separate panels of beautifully textured Lattice Stitch and using the intarsia method to create the abstract herringbone pattern, this bright and colourful cushion is sure to brighten up any corner of your home.

HOOK

5mm and 6mm Tunisian hook

5mm (US H8) regular crochet hook

YARN

DK (8-ply) cotton yarn in the following colours:

A Cream – 150g

B Turquoise – 50g

C Lime – 50g

D Pink – 50g

E Yellow – 50g

F Purple – 50g

G Light blue – 50g

H Coral – 50g

I Melon – 50g

OTHER MATERIALS

One 30 x 45cm (12 x 18in) cushion insert

4 buttons

Pins

Yarn bobbins

SPECIAL STITCHES AND TECHNIQUES USED

Tunisian Simple Stitch (Tss): see Basic Stitches

Intarsia: see Colourwork

Tss2tog: insert hook under next 2 vertical bars, yo and pull up a lp (1 lp on hook)

FINISHED SIZE

30 x 45cm (12 x 18in)

FRONT

HERRINGBONE SECTION

Wind yarn bobbins: 3 with main colour and 1 each of contrast colours.

Foundation Row: Using Colour **A** and 5mm Tunisian hook, ch23. Pick up lp in second ch from hook and each ch to end. Return. (23 lps on hook)

Row 2: Using Colour **A**, Tss 6. Using Colour **B**, Tss 1. Using new bobbin of Colour **A**, Tss 13. Using Colour **C**, Tss 1, work end st. Return using corresponding colours.

Row 3: Using Colour **A**, Tss 5. Using Colour **B**, Tss 2. Using Colour **A**, Tss 12. Using Colour **C**, Tss 2, work end st. Return using corresponding colours.

Row 4: Using Colour **A**, Tss 4. Using Colour **B**, Tss 3. Using Colour **A**, Tss 11. Using Colour **C**, Tss 3, work end st. Return using corresponding colours.

Row 5: Using Colour **A**, Tss 3. Using Colour **B**, Tss 4. Using Colour **A**, Tss 10. Using Colour **C**, Tss 4, work end st. Return using corresponding colours.

Row 6: Using Colour **A**, Tss 2. Using Colour **B**, Tss 5. Using Colour **A**, Tss 9. Using Colour **C**, Tss 5, work end st. Return using corresponding colours.

Row 7: Using Colour **A**, Tss 1. Using Colour **B**, Tss 6. Using Colour **A**, Tss 8. Using Colour **C**, Tss 6, work end st. Return using corresponding colours, yo with Colour **B** on last st st.

Row 8: Using Colour **B**, Tss 7. Using Colour **A**, Tss 7. Using Colour **C**, Tss 7, work end st. Return using corresponding colours.

Row 9: Using Colour **B**, Tss 6. Using new bobbin of Colour **A**, Tss 1. Using Colour **D**, Tss 1. Using Colour **A**, Tss 6. Using Colour **C**, Tss 6. Using new bobbin of Colour **A**, Tss 1, work end st. Return using corresponding colours.

Row 10: Using Colour **B**, Tss 5. Using Colour **A**, Tss 2. Using Colour **D**, Tss 2. Using Colour **A**, Tss 5. Using Colour **C**, Tss 5. Using Colour **A**, Tss 2, work end st. Return using corresponding colours.

Row 11: Using Colour **B**, Tss 4. Using Colour **A**, Tss 3. Using Colour **D**, Tss 3. Using Colour **A**, Tss 4. Using Colour **C**, Tss 4. Using Colour **A**, Tss 3, work end st. Return using corresponding colours.

Row 12: Using Colour **B**, Tss 3. Using Colour **A**, Tss 4. Using Colour **D**, Tss 4. Using Colour **A**, Tss 3. Using Colour **C**, Tss 3. Using Colour **A**, Tss 4, work end st. Return using corresponding colours.

Row 13: Using Colour **B**, Tss 2. Using Colour **A**, Tss 5. Using Colour **D**, Tss 5. Using Colour **A**, Tss 2. Using Colour **C**, Tss 2. Using Colour **A**, Tss 5, work end st. Return using corresponding colours.

Row 14: Using Colour **B**, Tss 1. Using Colour **A**, Tss 6. Using Colour **D**, Tss 6. Using Colour **A**, Tss 1. Using Colour **C**, Tss 1. Using Colour **A**, Tss 6, work end st. Return using corresponding colours.

Row 15: Using Colour **A**, Tss 7. Using Colour **D**, Tss 7. Using Colour **A**, Tss 7, work end st. Return using corresponding colours.

Rows 16-56: Continue pattern, working from colourwork chart from Row 16 upwards, reading chart right to left and remembering that the first square is the first stitch already on the hook.

Bind off with Colour **A**.

COLOURWORK CHART

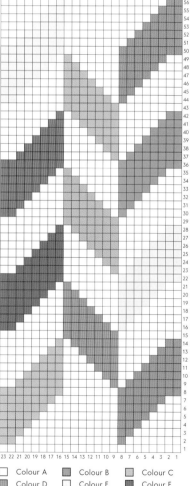

	Colour A		Colour B		Colour C
	Colour D		Colour E		Colour F
	Colour G		Colour H		Colour I

RIGHT SECTION

Change to 6mm Tunisian hook.

Foundation Row: Using colour **A**, join with a ss into first st in foundation row of Herringbone section and pick up 56 sts along the side of the herringbone section. Return (57 lps on hook).

Row 2: *Tss2tog, go back and Tss into first of these 2 bars. Repeat from * to last 2 sts, Tss 1, work end st. Return.

Row 3: Tss 1, *Tss2tog, go back and Tss into first of these 2 bars. Repeat from * to last s, work end st. Return. These 2 rows form pattern.

Rows 4-17: Repeat Rows 2 and 3. Bind off.

RIGHT AND LEFT SECTIONS CHART

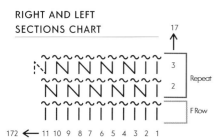

LEFT SECTION

Foundation Row: Work as for right section.

Rows 2-41: Work following pattern as set for right section.

BACK

BOTTOM SECTION

Foundation Row: Using Colour **B** and 6mm Tunisian hook, ch 50. Insert hook in second ch from hook, yo and pull up lp, leaving lp on hook; repeat for each ch to end (50 lps on hook). Return.

Rows 2-3: Tss to end. Return, changing to Colour **A** on last st of final return.

Row 4: Tss to end. Return, changing to Colour **D** on last st.

Rows 5-6: Tss to end. Return, changing to Colour **A** on last st of final return.

Row 7: Tss to end. Return, changing to Colour **C** on last st.

Rows 8-9: Tss to end. Return, changing to Colour **A** on last st of final return.

Row 10: Tss to end. Return, changing to Colour **F** on last st.

Rows 11-12: Tss to end. Return, changing to Colour **A** on last st of final return.

Row 13: Tss to end. Return, changing to Colour **G** on last st.

Rows 14-15: Tss to end. Return, changing to Colour **A** on last st of final return.

Row 16: Tss to end. Return, changing to Colour **H** on last st.

Rows 17-18: Tss to end. Return, changing to Colour **A** on last st of final return.

Row 19: Tss to end. Return, changing to Colour **E** on last st.

Rows 20-21: Tss to end. Return, changing to Colour **A** on last st of final return.

Row 22: Tss to end. Return, changing to Colour **I** on last st.

Rows 23-24: Tss to end. Return, changing to Colour **A** on last st of final return.

Row 25: Tss to end. Return, changing to Colour **B** on last st.

Rows 26-27: Tss to end. Return, changing to Colour **A** on last st of final return.

Row 28: Tss to end. Return, changing to Colour **D** on last st.

Rows 29-30: Tss to end. Return, changing to Colour **A** on last st of final return.

Row 31: Tss to end. Return, changing to Colour **C** on last st.

Rows 32-33: Tss to end. Return, changing to Colour **A** on last st of final return.

Row 34: Tss to end. Return, changing to Colour **F** on last st.

Rows 35-36: Tss to end. Return, changing to Colour **A** on last st of final return.

Row 37: Tss to end. Return, changing to Colour **G** on last st.

Rows 38-39: Tss to end. Return, changing to Colour **A** on last st of final return.

Row 40: Tss to end. Return, changing to Colour **H** on last st.

Rows 41-42: Tss to end. Return, changing to Colour **A** on last st of final return.

Row 43: Tss to end. Return, changing to Colour **E** on last st.

Rows 44-45: Tss to end. Return, changing to Colour **A** on last st of final return.

Row 46: Tss to end. Return, changing to Colour **I** on last st.

Rows 47-48: Tss to end. Return, changing to Colour **A** on last st of final return.

Row 49: Tss to end. Return, changing to Colour **B** on last st.

Rows 50-51: Tss to end. Return, changing to Colour **A** on last st of final return.

Row 52: Tss to end. Return, changing to Colour **D** on last st.

Rows 53-54: Tss to end. Return, changing to Colour **A** on last st of final return.

Row 55: Tss to end. Return, changing to Colour **C** on last st.

Rows 56-57: Tss to end. Return, changing to Colour **A** on last st of final return.

Row 58: Tss to end. Return, changing to Colour **G** on last st.

Rows 59-60: Tss to end. Return, changing to Colour **A** on last st of final return.

Row 61: Tss to end. Return. Bind off.

TOP SECTION

Foundation Row: Using Colour **B** and 6mm Tunisian hook, ch 50. Insert hook in second ch from hook, yo and pull up lp, leaving lp on hook; repeat for each ch to end (50 lps on hook). Return.

Rows 2-3: Tss to end. Return, changing to Colour **A** on last st of final return.

Row 4: Tss to end. Return, changing to Colour **D** on last st.

Rows 5-6: Tss to end. Return, changing to Colour **A** on last st of final return.

Row 7: Tss to end. Return, changing to Colour **C** on last st.

Rows 8-9: Tss to end. Return, changing to Colour **A** on last st of final return.

Row 10: Tss to end. Return, changing to Colour **F** on last st.

Rows 11-12: Tss to end. Return, changing to Colour **A** on last st of final return.

Row 13: Tss to end. Return, changing to Colour **G** on last st.

Rows 14-15: Tss to end. Return, changing to Colour **A** on last st of final return.

Row 16: Tss to end. Return, changing to Colour **H** on last st.

Rows 17-18: Tss to end. Return, changing to Colour **A** on last st of final return.

Row 19: Tss to end. Return, changing to Colour **E** on last st.

Rows 20-21: Tss to end. Return, changing to Colour **A** on last st of final return.

Row 22: Tss to end. Return, changing to Colour **I** on last st.

Row 23: Tss to end. Return.

Row 24: Tks in next 8 sts, *sk next 2 sts, Tks 8. Repeat from * to last st, work end st. Return as normal up to skipped sts, **ch 2, continue return pass up to next skipped sts, repeat from ** to end.

Row 25: Tss in each st up to buttonhole, *pick up lp in next 2 ch, Tss up to next buttonhole. Repeat from * to last st, work end st. Return. Bind off.

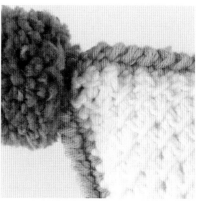

FINISHING

With wrong sides together, lay top and bottom back sections onto front piece, overlapping the top back section approximately 3cm (1 1/8in) over the bottom section.

Pin in place.

EDGING

Row 1: Using 5mm crochet hook and Colour **D**, join all pieces working a sc into each st, working through all layers around the edge of the cushion. Join with a ss into first sc. Don't turn.

Row 2: Ch 1 (not counted as st), work in Crab st to end. Join with a ss into first ch and fasten off.

Weave ends in and sew buttons on.

NOTE

YOU CAN ALSO MAKE 4 POM POMS WITH THE LEFTOVER YARN AND ATTACH ONE TO EACH CORNER.

CHERRY POTHOLDER

Not only will this cute little potholder jazz up your kitchen, this easy project also gives you the opportunity to try out a number of different techniques such as changing colours, cross stitch, mitered squares and joining-as-you-go.

HOOK

5mm straight Tunisian hook

4mm regular crochet hook

YARN

DK (8-ply) cotton yarn in the following colours:

A Turquoise – 50g

B Light Blue – 50g

C Red – 25g

Scraps of green and pink for cross stitch accents

OTHER MATERIALS

Wool tapestry needle

SPECIAL STITCHES AND TECHNIQUES USED

Tunisian Simple Stitch (Tss): see Basic Stitches

Decrease: see Techniques

Slip stitch (sl st): see Techniques

Single crochet (sc): see Techniques

Crab stitch: see Techniques

FINISHED SIZE

20 x 20cm (8 x 8in)

CROSS STITCH CHART

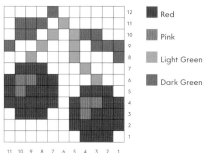

■ Red
▨ Pink
▩ Light Green
▨ Dark Green

CHERRY MOTIF

Working from chart, and referring to Cross Stitch instructions in the Embellishments section, embroider the design into the bottom right hand corner of the front piece.

BACK

SQUARE ONE

Foundation Row: Using Colour **A**, ch 37. Pick up a loop from back bump in 2nd ch from hook, and in each ch to end, leaving all loops on hook. Return.

Row 2: Tss 16, Tss3tog, place marker on middle st of decrease just made, Tss 16, work end st. Return (35 lps)

Row 3: Tss 15, Tss3tog, Tss 15, work end st. Return. (33 lps)

Row 4: Tss 14, Tss3tog, Tss 14, work end st. Return. (31 lps)

Row 5: Tss 13, Tss3tog, Tss 13, work end st. Return. (29 lps)

Row 6: Tss 12, Tss3tog, Tss 12, work end st. Return. (27 lps)

Row 7: Tss 11, Tss3tog, Tss 11, work end st. Return. (25 lps)

Row 8: Tss 10, Tss3tog, Tss 10, work end st. Return. (23 lps)

Row 9: Tss 9, Tss3tog, Tss 9, work end st. Return. (21 lps)

Row 10: Tss 8, Tss3tog, Tss 8, work end st. Return. (19 lps)

Row 11: Tss 7, Tss3tog, Tss 7, work end st. Return. (17 lps)

Row 12: Tss 6, Tss3tog, Tss 6, work end st. Return. (15 lps)

Row 13: Tss 5, Tss3tog, Tss 5, work end st. Return. (13 lps)

Row 14: Tss 4, Tss3tog, Tss 4, work end st. Return. (11 lps)

Row 15: Tss 3, Tss3tog, Tss 3, work end st. Return. (9 lps)

Row 16: Tss 2, Tss3tog, Tss 2, work end st. Return. (7 lps)

Row 17: Tss 1, Tss3tog, Tss 1, work end st. Return. (5 lps)

Row 18: Tss3tog, work end st. Return with a yo and through all 3 lps on hook. Yo through last lp on hook and fasten off.

FRONT

Foundation Row: Using Colour **A**, ch 36. Pick up a loop from back bump in 2nd ch from hook, and in each ch to end, leaving all loops on hook. Return.

Rows 2- 3: Continuing with Colour **A**, Tss to last st, work end st. Return. Change to Colour **B** on last 2 lps of return in Row 3.

Rows 4–5: Continuing with Colour **B**, Tss to last st, work end st. Return. Change to Colour **A** on last 2 lps of return in Row 5.

Rows 6–34: Repeat Rows 2–5. Bind off.

WORK SQUARES IN THIS ORDER:

2	3
1	4

SQUARE TWO

Foundation Row: With a slip knot on your hook in Colour **B**, join to first square at marker, ch 19. Pick up a loop from back bump in 2nd ch from hook, and in each ch to end, then pick up 18 sts along the edge of Square One (37 lps on hook). Return.

Rows 2–18: Work as for Square One.

SQUARE THREE

Using Colour **A**, work as for Square Two, joining yarn at the same point and picking up sts along the edge of Square Two.

SQUARE FOUR

Using Colour **B**, pick up 18 sts along edge of Square One, pick up 1 st at the intersection where all squares meet, pick up 18 sts along edge of Square Three (37 lps on hook). Return.

Rows 2–18: Work as for Square One.

FINISHING

Switch to 4mm crochet hook. Lay front and back pieces with wrong sides together, right sides facing out.

Round 1: Join Colour **C** with a ss through both layers of any corner, *3 sc into same st, continuing to work through both layers, sc into each st along to next corner. Repeat from * to end. Join with a ss into first sc.

Round 2: Ch 1 (not counted as st), work in Crab st to end. Join with a ss into first ch-1. Make hanging loop: Ch 15, join with a ss into first ch, sc 15 into chain loop. Fasten off.

Weave ends in.

POTHOLDER MITRED SQUARE CHART

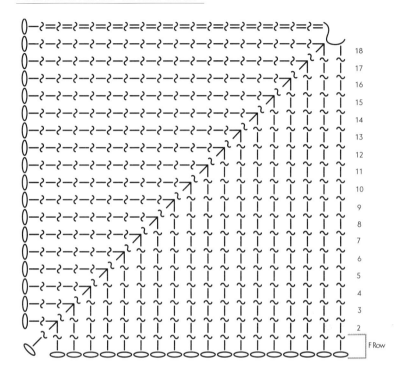

GEOMETRIC WALL HANGING

The woven fabric created by Tunisian crochet lends itself beautifully to creating stunning artwork for your home. Practice your colourwork skills by creating this simple geometric design with the Intarsia method as well as adding an extra dimension to your stitches with the 2-tone Simple stitch.

HOOK

5mm straight Tunisian hook

YARN

DK (8-ply) cotton yarn in the following colours:

A Cream – 30g

B Aqua – 25g

C Mint – 25g

D Yellow – 25g

E Coral – 25g

OTHER MATERIALS

40cm x 12mm (16 x $^1/_2$in) wooden dowel

80cm x 5mm (31$^1/_2$in x $^1/_4$in) rope or cord

SPECIAL STITCHES AND TECHNIQUES USED

Tunisian Simple Stitch (Tss): see Basic Stitches

M1bb (Make 1 – back bump): pick up a loop from the back bump of the return chain behind the next vertical bar (1 st increased)

Note: *The next stitch in pattern is then worked into same vertical bar*

FINISHED SIZE:

30 x 42cm (12 x 16$^1/_2$in)

WALL HANGING

Foundation Row: Using Colour **A**, ch 2. Pick up a loop from the top loop of 2nd ch from hook, and also from the back bump of same ch, leaving all loops on hook (3 lps). Return using Colour **B**.

Row 2: Continuing with Colour **B**, M1bb, Tss 1, M1bb, work end st (5 lps). Return using Colour **A**.

Row 3: Continuing with Colour **A**, M1bb, Tss 3, M1bb, work end st (7 lps). Return using Colour **B**.

Row 4: Continuing with Colour **B**, M1bb, Tss 5, M1bb, work end st (9 lps). Return using Colour **A**.

Row 5: Continuing with Colour **A**, M1bb, Tss 7, M1bb, work end st (11 lps). Return using Colour **B**.

Row 6: Continuing with Colour **B**, M1bb, Tss 9, M1bb, work end st (13 lps). Return using Colour **A**.

Row 7: Continuing with Colour **A**, M1bb, Tss 11, M1bb, work end st (15 lps). Return using Colour **B**.

Row 8: Continuing with Colour **B**, M1bb, Tss 13, M1bb, work end st (17 lps). Return using Colour **A**.

Row 9: Continuing with Colour **A**, M1bb, Tss 15, M1bb, work end st (19 lps). Return using Colour **B**.

Row 10: Continuing with Colour **B**, M1bb, Tss 17, M1bb, workend st (21 lps) Return using Colour **A**.

Row 11: Continuing with Colour **A**, M1bb, Tss 19, M1bb, work end st (23 lps). Return using Colour **D**.

Row 12: Continuing with Colour **D**, M1bb, Tss 21, M1bb, work end st (25 lps). Return using Colour **A**.

Row 13: Continuing with Colour **A**, M1bb, Tss 23, M1bb, work end st (27 lps). Return using Colour **D**.

Row 14: Continuing with Colour **D**, M1bb, Tss 25, M1bb, work end st (29 lps). Return using Colour **A**.

Row 15: Continuing with Colour **A**, M1bb, Tss 27, M1bb, work end st (31 lps). Return using Colour **D**.

Row 16: Continuing with Colour **D**, M1bb, Tss 29, M1bb, work end st (33 lps). Return using Colour **A**.

Row 17: Continuing with Colour **A**, M1bb, Tss 31, M1bb, work end st (35 lps). Return using Colour **D**.

Row 18: Continuing with Colour **D**, M1bb, Tss 33, M1bb, work end st (37 lps). Return using Colour **A** .

Row 19: Continuing with Colour **A**, M1bb, Tss 35, M1bb, work end st (39 lps). Return using Colour **D**.

Row 20: Continuing with Colour **D**, M1bb, Tss 37, M1bb, work end st (41 lps). Return using Colour **A**.

Row 21: Continuing with Colour **A**, M1bb, Tss 39, M1bb, work end st (43 lps). Return using Colour **E**.

Row 22: Continuing with Colour **E**, M1bb, Tss 41, M1bb, work end st (45 lps). Return using Colour **A**.

Row 23: Continuing with Colour **A**, M1bb, Tss 43, M1bb, work end st (47 lps). Return using Colour **E**.

Row 24: Continuing with Colour **E**, M1bb, Tss 45, M1bb, work end st (49 lps). Return using Colour **A**.

Row 25: Continuing with Colour **A**, M1bb, Tss 47, M1bb, work end st (51 lps). Return using Colour **E**.

Row 26: Continuing with Colour **E**, M1bb, Tss 49, M1bb, work end st (53 lps). Return using Colour **A**.

Row 27: Continuing with Colour **A**, M1bb, Tss 51, M1bb, work end st (55 lps). Return using Colour **E**.

Row 28: Continuing with Colour **E**, M1bb, Tss 53, M1bb, work end st (57 lps). Return using Colour **A**.

Row 29: Continuing with Colour **A**, M1bb, Tss 55, M1bb, work end st (59 lps). Return using Colour **E**.

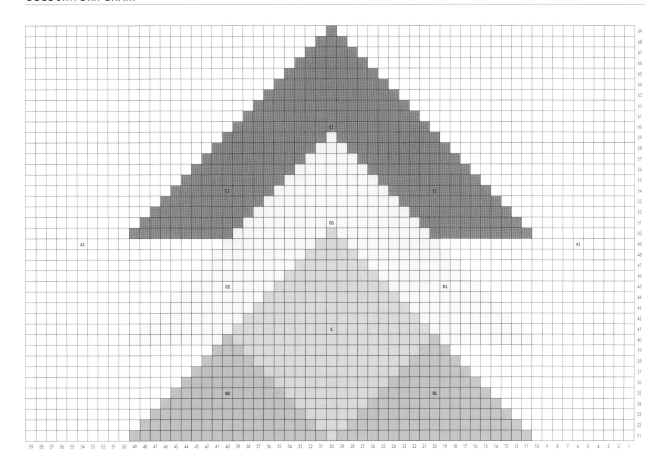

Row 30: Continuing with Colour **E**, Tss 57, work end st. Return using Colour **A**.

Rows 31-69: Before beginning intarsia design, wind all colours except for Colour **C** into two separate balls or bobbins.

Begin working from chart reading right to left and bottom to top.

Rows 70-84: Using Colour **A**, Tss 57, work end st. Return.

Bind off. Fasten off, leaving a long tail of approximately 60cm (23½in) for sewing hanging rod pocket.

Weave ends in.

A1	Colour A – 1st bobbin	D1	Colour D – 1st bobbin
A2	Colour A – 2nd bobbin	D2	Colour D – 2nd bobbin
B1	Colour B – 1st bobbin	E1	Colour E – 1st bobbin
B2	Colour B – 2nd bobbin	E2	Colour D – 2nd bobbin
C	Colour C		

HANGING ROD POCKET

Along the top of the piece, fold approximately 3cm (1¹/₈in) of fabric to the back and pin in place. Whip stitch the edge to the back of the wall hanging and thread the wooden dowel through the pocket.

HANGER

Cut a piece of rope 80cm (31¹/₂in) long.

Fold back one end by approximately 13cm (5in) to form a loop and wrap with tape to hold in place.

Cut various lengths of leftover contrast coloured yarns.

Make sure there is enough space for your hanging rod to fit through and then working from the loop, wind your contrast yarn as tightly as you can around the rope and the tail end, winding over the tail end to hide it. When you finish the first colour, cut the yarn and thread the end onto a tapestry needle, then work the needle back down through the wrapped yarn as far as you can go before cutting off as close as possible.

Keep winding with other colours until the wraps measure approximately 5cm (2in).

Repeat for the other end of the hanging loop.

TASSEL

Take a strand of each of your colours and wrap 10 times around an 8cm (3in) piece of cardboard.

Thread one separate strand of any colour under the top of your wrapped yarn. Tie a tight knot to secure. Cut this yarn, leaving long tails to use to attach later.

Slide yarn off cardboard. With the same colour yarn you used to tie off, tie another knot approximately 1.5cm (¹/₂in) down from the top and wrap it around the tassel head 5-6 times. Thread the tail end onto a tapestry needle and work the needle back down through the wrapped yarn.

Trim the tassel ends evenly.

Using the tail ends of the top knot attach to the bottom point of the wall hanging.

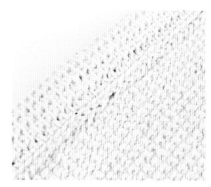

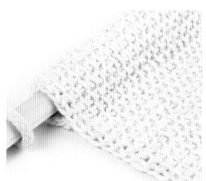

CHEVRON CUSHION

There is something very soothing about creating rows of zig zags. Simple increases and decreases create this striking pattern and the colour blocking creates a modern aesthetic. Many different looks can be achieved with this stitch pattern by changing the width of the stripes and your use of colour.

HOOK

5mm Tunisian hook with 40cm (16in) cable, or a straight Tunisian hook can also be used.

5mm (US H8) regular crochet hook

YARN

DK (8-ply) cotton yarn in the following colours:

A Aqua – 50g

B Mint – 50g

C Medium Pink – 50g

D Light Pink – 50g

E Denim Blue – 50g

F Light Blue – 50g

OTHER MATERIALS

45cm (18in) cushion insert

6 x 18mm (³/₄in) buttons

Sewing needle and thread

SPECIAL STITCHES AND TECHNIQUES USED

Tunisian Simple Stitch (Tss): see Basic stitches

Tunisian Double crochet (Tdc): see Basic stitches

M1tb (make 1 – top bar): insert hook under top loop of horizontal bar before next st, yo, pull up loop and leave on hook

Tss3tog: insert hook under next 3 sts, yo and pull up loop (1 loop on hook)

Tdc3tog: yo, insert hook under next 3 sts, yo and pull up a loop, yo, pull through 2 lps on hook

Tunisian Slip Stitch (Tsl): pick up stitch onto hook without working

FINISHED SIZE

45 x 45cm (18 x 18in)

FRONT

Foundation Row: Using Colour **A**, ch 97. Pick up a loop from back bump in 2nd ch from hook, and in each ch to end, leaving all loops on hook. Return.

Row 2: *M1tb, Tss 6, Tss3tog, Tss 6, M1tb, Tss 1. Repeat from * to last st, replacing last Tss1 with an end st. Return. Repeat Row 2 for remaining rows following the colour sequence as indicated below

Rows 3-4: Continue with Colour **A**, changing to Colour **B** on the last 2 lps of return in Row 4. Don't cut Colour **A** yet.

Rows 5-6: Work in Colour **B**, changing back to Colour **A** on the last 2 lps of return in Row 6. Don't cut Colour **B** yet.

Rows 7-8: Work in Colour **A**, changing back to Colour **B** on the last 2 lps of return in Row 8. Don't cut Colour **A** yet.

Rows 9-10: Work in Colour **B**, changing back to Colour **A** on the last 2 lps of return in Row 10. Don't cut Colour **B** yet.

Rows 11-12: Work in Colour **A**, changing back to Colour **B** on the last 2 lps of return in Row 12. Fasten off Colour **A**.

Rows 13-16: Work in Colour **B**, changing to Colour **C** on the last 2 lps of return in Row 16. Don't cut Colour **B** yet.

Rows 17-18: Work in Colour **C**, changing back to Colour **B** on the last 2 lps of return in Row 18. Don't cut Colour **C** yet.

Rows 19-20: Work in Colour **B**, changing back to Colour **C** on the last 2 lps of return in Row 20. Fasten off Colour **B**.

Rows 21-22: Work in Colour **C**, changing to Colour **D** on the last 2 lps of return in Row 22. Don't cut Colour **C** yet.

Rows 23-24: Work in Colour **D**, changing back to Colour **C** on the last 2 lps of return in Row 24. Don't cut Colour **D** yet.

Rows 25-28: Work in Colour **C**, changing back to Colour **D** on the last 2 lps of return in Row 28. Don't cut Colour **C** yet.

Rows 29-30: Work in Colour **D**, changing back to Colour **C** on the last 2 lps of return in Row 30. Don't cut Colour **D** yet.

Rows 31-32: Work in Colour **C**, changing back to Colour **D** on the last 2 lps of return in Row 32. Fasten off Colour **C**.

Rows 33-36: Work in Colour **D**, changing to Colour **E** on the last 2 lps of return in Row 36. Don't cut Colour **D** yet.

Rows 37-38: Work in Colour **E**, changing back to Colour **D** on the last 2 lps of return in Row 38. Don't cut Colour **E** yet.

Rows 39-40: Work in Colour **D**, changing to Colour **E** on the last 2 lps of return in Row 40. Fasten off Colour **D**.

Rows 41-42: Work in Colour **E**, changing to Colour **F** on the last 2 lps of return in Row 42. Don't cut Colour **E** yet.

Rows 43-44: Work in Colour **F**, changing back to Colour **E** on the last 2 lps of return in Row 44. Don't cut Colour **F** yet.

Rows 45-48: Work in Colour **E**, changing back to Colour **F** on the last 2 lps of return in Row 48. Don't cut Colour **E** yet.

Rows 49-50: Work in Colour **F**, changing back to Colour **E** on the last 2 lps of return in Row 50. Don't cut Colour **F** yet.

Rows 51-52: Work in Colour **E**, changing back to Colour **F** on the last 2 lps of return in Row 52. Fasten off Colour **E**.

Rows 53-54: Work in Colour **F**.

Bind off loosely.

PATTERN REPEAT CHART

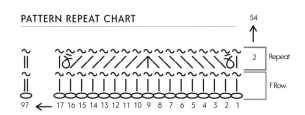

CHEVRON CUSHION

STRAIGHTEN TOP

The following straightening rows will use the entrelac method. As you will only have 10 stitches on your hook at a time you may find it more comfortable to work with a regular crochet hook.

Join Colour **E** with a sl st to top right hand edge and work as follows:

Row 1: Pick up 7 loops down peak edge and 1 loop from edge of next peak (9 lps on hook). **Return:** yo, pull through 2 lps up to last 3 lps, yo pull through 3 lps.

Row 2: Skip next st, Tss next 6 sts and pick up 1 loop from edge of next peak (8 lps on hook). **Return:** yo, pull through 2 lps up to last 3 lps, yo pull through 3 lps.

Row 3: Skip next st, Tss next 5 sts and pick up 1 loop from edge of next peak (7 lps on hook). **Return:** yo, pull through 2 lps up to last 3 lps, yo pull through 3 lps.

Row 4: Skip next st, Tss next 4 sts and pick up 1 loop from edge of next peak (6 lps on hook). **Return:** yo, pull through 2 lps up to last 3 lps, yo pull through 3 lps.

Row 5: Skip next st, Tss next 3 sts and pick up 1 loop from edge of next peak (5 lps on hook). **Return:** yo, pull through 2 lps up to last 3 lps, yo pull through 3 lps.

Row 6: Skip next st, Tss next 2 sts and pick up 1 loop from edge of next peak (4 lps on hook). **Return:** yo, pull through 2 lps up to last 3 lps, yo pull through 3 lps.

Row 7: Skip next st, Tss 1 and pick up 1 loop from edge of next peak (3 lps on hook). **Return:** yo pull through 3 lps. Sl st back into same sp and into next st.

Repeat Rows 1-7 for remaining 5 gaps.

Finish off cushion edge by working 1 sc into each stitch along the top edge and fasten off.

NOTE

IN ROW 1 YOU'LL PICK UP 7 LOOPS AND THEN SKIP ONE STITCH BEFORE PICKING UP THE NEXT STITCH ON THE EDGE OF THE NEXT PEAK – THIS IS CORRECT.

STRAIGHTEN BOTTOM

Turn work upside down and join Colour **B** with a sl st to the lower outside edge of the first chevron. Fill in the gaps as follows:

FIRST ½ TRIANGLE

Row 1: Pick up 7 loops along edge (8 lps on hook). Return.

Row 2: Skip next st, Tss 4, sk 1, work end st (6 lps on hook). Return.

Row 3: Skip next st, Tss 2, sk 1, work end st (4 lps on hook). Return.

Row 4: Tss2tog, work end st (3 lps on hook). **Return:** yo, draw through 3 lps on hook.

Work 3 sl st along edge to top of next peak

STRAIGHT EDGE TRIANGLES

Row 1: Pick up 7 loops down peak edge and 1 loop from edge of next peak (9 lps on hook). **Return:** yo, pull through 2 lps up to last 3 lps, yo pull through 3 lps.

Row 2: Skip next st, Tss next 6 sts and pick up 1 loop from edge of next peak (8 lps on hook). **Return:** yo, pull through 2 lps up to last 3 lps, yo pull through 3 lps.

Row 3: Skip next st, Tss next 5 sts and pick up 1 loop from edge of next peak (7 lps on hook). **Return:** yo, pull through 2 lps up to last 3 lps, yo pull through 3 lps.

Row 4: Skip next st, Tss next 4 sts and pick up 1 loop from edge of next peak (6 lps on hook). **Return:** yo, pull through 2 lps up to last 3 lps, yo pull through 3 lps.

Row 5: Skip next st, Tss next 3 sts and pick up 1 loop from edge of next peak (5 lps on hook). **Return:** yo, pull through 2 lps up to last 3 lps, yo pull through 3 lps.

Row 6: Skip next st, Tss next 2 sts and pick up 1 loop from edge of next peak (4 lps on hook). **Return:** yo, pull through 2 lps up to last 3 lps, yo pull through 3 lps.

Row 7: Skip next st, Tss 1 and pick up 1 loop from edge of next peak (3 lps on hook). **Return:** yo pull through 3 lps. Sl st back into same sp and into next st.

Repeat Rows 1–7 for the remaining 4 gaps.

END ½ TRIANGLE

Row 1: Pick up 7 lps along edge (8 lps on hook). Return.

Row 2: Tss 5, sk 1, work end st (7 lps on hook). **Return:** yo, pull through 3 lps, yo pull through 2 lps to end.

Row 3: Tss 4, sk 1, work end st (6 lps on hook). **Return:** yo, pull through 3 lps, yo, pull through 2 lps to end.

Finish off cushion edge by working 1 sc into each stitch along the top edge and fasten off.

BACK

BOTTOM HALF

Work as for Front up to Row 40. Don't change colour at end of row.

Row 41: Straighten top – Continuing in Colour **D**, *Tss 3, Tdc 3, Tdc3tog, Tdc 3, Tss 3, Tsl. Repeat from * to last st replacing last Tsl with an end st. Return.
Bind off.

STRAIGHTEN BOTTOM

Work as for Front.

TOP HALF

Foundation Row: Using Colour **E**, ch 97. Pick up a loop from back bump in 2nd ch from hook, and in each ch to end, leaving all loops on hook. Return.

Rows 2-18: Work as for Front starting from Row 38 through to Row 54.
Bind off.

STRAIGHTEN TOP

Work as for Front.

BUTTON LOOPS

Using your 5mm crochet hook join Colour **E** with a sl st to the middle stitch of the first peak, ch 6, sl st back into beginning ch to form a loop.

Fasten off and repeat for remaining 5 peaks.

FINISHING

Weave ends in.

With right sides together, lay top and bottom back sections onto front piece, overlapping the back bottom section approximately 3cm (1¹/₈in) over the back top section. Pin in place.

Using 5mm crochet hook and any colour, join the pieces together with a sl st worked into each st and through all layers around the cushion.

Turn cushion the right way out. Sew buttons on and place cushion insert inside cover.

PINEAPPLE PINCUSHION

Everybody needs a pineapple pincushion in their life! Add a bit of fun to your sewing kit with this cute 3-D pineapple motif.

▶▶▶▶◀◀◀◀

HOOK

5mm straight Tunisian hook

4mm crochet hook

YARN

DK (8-ply) cotton yarn in the following colours:

A Pink – 50g

B Yellow – 50g

C Green – 20g

OTHER MATERIALS

Stuffing

SPECIAL STITCHES AND TECHNIQUES USED

Tunisian Knit stitch (Tks): see Basic Stitches

Puff Stitch: Insert hook under front and back bar of next st, yo, pull up loop, *yo, insert hook back under same st, yo pull up loop. Repeat from * twice more (7 lps on hook), yo pull through 7 loops

Single crochet (sc): see Techniques

Half Double crochet (hdc): see Techniques

Crab st: see Techniques

FINISHED SIZE

12 x 12cm (5 x 5in)

NOTE

ONCE YOU START WORKING THE PINEAPPLE DESIGN, YOU WILL NEED 2 SEPARATE LOTS OF COLOUR A. YOU CAN EITHER USE A STRAND FROM BOTH THE CENTRE AND FROM THE OUTSIDE OF THE BALL OR, ALTERNATIVELY, WIND 2 SEPARATE BALLS BEFORE STARTING.

FRONT

Foundation Row: Using Colour **A**, ch 21. Pick up a loop from back bump in 2nd ch from hook, and in each ch to end, leaving all loops on hook. Return.

Rows 2–7: Tks to last st, work end st. Return.

Work from chart or written instructions for Rows 8–15.

Row 8: Using Colour **A** #1 Tks 8, using Colour **B** make 3 Puff sts, using Colour **A** #2 Tks 8, work end st. Return using corresponding yarns.

Row 9: Using Colour **A** #1 Tks 7, using Colour **B**, puff st, (Tks 1, puff st) twice, using Colour **A** #2 Tks 7, work end st. Return using corresponding yarns.

Row 10: Using Colour **A** #1 Tks 6, using Colour **B**, puff st, (Tks 1, puff st) three times, using Colour **A** #2 Tks 6, work end st. Return using corresponding yarns.

Row 11: Using Colour **A** #1 Tks 5, using Colour **B**, puff st, (Tks 1, puff st) four times, using Colour **A** #2 Tks 5, work end st. Return using corresponding yarns.

Row 12: Using Colour **A** #1 Tks 5, using Colour **B**, Tks 1, (puff st, Tks 1) four times, using Colour **A** #2 Tks 5, work end st. Return using corresponding yarns.

Row 13: Using Colour **A** #1 Tks 5, using Colour **B**, puff st, (Tks 1, puff st) four times, using Colour **A** #2 Tks 5, work end st. Return using corresponding yarns.

Row 14: Using Colour **A** #1 Tks 6, using Colour **B**, puff st, (Tks 1, puff st) three times, using Colour **A** #2 Tks 6, work end st. Return using corresponding yarns.

Row 15: Using Colour **A** #1 Tks 7, using Colour **B**, puff st, (Tks 1, puff st) twice, using Colour **A** #2 Tks 7, work end st. Return using corresponding yarns.

Fasten off Colour **B** and Colour **A** #2.

Rows 16–24: Using Colour **A** Tks to last st, work end st. Return.

Bind off

PINEAPPLE PINCUSHION CHART

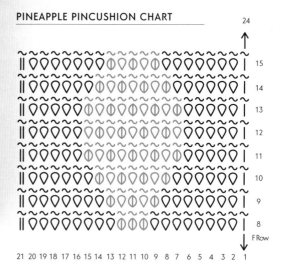

LEAVES

Switch to 4mm crochet hook.

Join Colour **C** with a sl st worked under both bars of first puff st from Row 15, *ch 5, starting in 2nd ch from hook, work 1 sc then 3 hdc. Sl st under both bars of next Tks. Repeat from *. Sl st under both bars of last puff st and work another leaf the same. Join with a sl st in same sp.

Fasten off and thread loose ends through to wrong side.

Weave in ends.

BACK

Foundation Row: Using Colour **A**, ch 21. Pick up a loop from back bump in 2nd ch from hook, and in each ch to end, leaving all loops on hook. Return.

Row 2: Tks to last st, work end st. Return, changing to Colour **B** on last 2 lps.

Rows 3–4: Continuing in Colour **B**, Tks to last st, work end st. Return, changing to Colour **A** on last 2 lps of final return.

Rows 5–24: Work as for Rows 3–4, changing colours every 2 rows. Bind off.

FINISHING

Switch to 4mm crochet hook.

Lay front and back pieces with wrong sides together and right sides facing out.

Round 1: Using 4mm crochet hook and Colour **B**, join pieces together working a sc into each st and through both layers around three sides. Stuff firmly, then finish joining in the same way as before. Join with a ss into first sc.

Round 2: Ch 1 (not counted as st), work in Crab st to end. Join with a ss into first ch. Fasten off.

Weave ends in.

PINEAPPLE PINCUSHION

OMBRE RUG

This ombre mat is an easy make and the perfect size to brighten up your kitchen or bathroom. Use four shades of any colour to suit your own space.

HOOK

6mm Tunisian hook with 60cm (23$\frac{1}{2}$in) cable

4.5mm crochet hook

YARN

Aran weight (10-ply) cotton yarn in the following colours:

A Dark Blue – 200g

B Turquoise – 200g

C Light Blue – 200g

D Very Light Blue – 50g

OTHER MATERIALS

Non-slip mat to fit

SPECIAL STITCHES AND TECHNIQUES USED

Tunisian Full Stitch (Tfs): see Basic stitches

Slip stitch (sl st): see Techniques

Single crochet (sc): see Techniques

Sc blo (regular single crochet – back loop only): insert hook under the back loop only of the stitch, yo and complete sc as normal

FINISHED SIZE

60 x 90cm (23$\frac{1}{2}$ x 35$\frac{1}{2}$in)

RUG

Foundation Row: Using Colour **A**, ch 80. Pick up a loop from back bump in 2nd ch from hook, and in each ch to end, leaving all loops on hook. Return.

Row 2: Tfs into sp between 2nd and 3rd sts and into each sp between sts to last st, work end st. Return.

Row 3: Tfs into sp between 1st and 2nd sts and into each sp between sts up to last sp, sk this sp, work end st. Return.

Rows 2 and 3 form Mesh stitch pattern.

Rows 4-15: Continuing in Colour **A**, repeat Rows 2 and 3.

Row 16: Continuing in Colour **A**, work as for Row 2, changing to Colour **B** on last 2 lps of return. Don't cut Colour **A**.

Row 17: Using Colour **B** work as for Row 3, changing back to Colour **A** on last 2 lps of return.

Rows 18-29: Continue working in pattern, alternating Colours **A** and **B** every row. Fasten off Colour **A** after Row 28.

Rows 30-43: Continuing in Colour **B**, work in pattern.

Row 44: Continuing in Colour **B**, work as for Row 2, changing to Colour **C** on last 2 lps of return. Don't cut Colour **B**.

Row 45: Using Colour **C** work as for Row 3, changing back to Colour **B** on last 2 lps of return.

Rows 46-57: Continue working in pattern, alternating Colours **B** and **C** every row. Fasten off Colour **B** after Row 56.

Rows 58-71: Continuing in Colour **C**, work in pattern.

Row 72: Continuing in Colour **C**, work as for Row 2, changing to Colour **D** on last 2 lps of return. Don't cut Colour **C**.

Row 73: Using Colour **D** work as for Row 3, changing back to Colour **C** on last 2 lps of return.

Rows 74-84: Continue working in pattern, alternating Colours **C** and **D** every row. Fasten off Colour **D** after Row 83.

Rows 85-98: Continuing in Colour **C**, work in pattern.

Row 99: Continuing in Colour **C**, work as for Row 2, changing to Colour **B** on last 2 lps of return. Don't cut Colour **C**.

RUG CHART

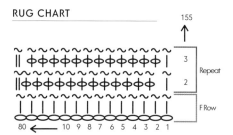

Row 100: Using Colour **B** work as for Row 3, changing back to Colour **C** on last 2 lps of return.

Rows 101-112: Continue working in pattern, alternating Colours **B** and **C** every row. Fasten off Colour **C** after Row 111.

Rows 113-126: Continuing in Colour **B**, work in pattern.

Row 127: Continuing in Colour **B**, work as for Row 2, changing to Colour **A** on last 2 lps of return. Don't cut Colour **B**.

Row 128: Using Colour **A** work as for Row 3, changing back to Colour **B** on last 2 lps of return.

Rows 129-140: Continue working in pattern, alternating Colours **A** and **B** every row. Fasten off Colour **B** after Row 139.

Rows 141-155: Continuing in Colour **B**, work in pattern.

Bind off.

NOTE

THE BORDER IS WORKED IN REGULAR CROCHET.

BORDER

Switch to 4.5mm crochet hook

Round 1: Join Colour **A** in any corner and sl st loosely into each st around rug to end. Join with a sl st and fasten off. Don't turn.

Round 2: All stitches in this round are worked under the top loop only of previous round's sl st. Join Colour **C** in any corner, ch 1 (not counted as st), *3 sc into same st (corner made), sc into each st up to next corner. Repeat from * to end. Join with a sl st and fasten off. Don't turn.

Round 3: Join Colour **A** into the middle st of any corner, ch 1 (not counted as st) *3 sc blo into same st (corner made), sc blo into each st up to next corner. Repeat from * to end. Join with a sl st and fasten off.

FINISHING

Weave ends in.

If your rug ends are curling, place a damp cloth over the rug and press with an iron. Leave to cool.

If your rug will be used on a wooden or tiled floor, be sure to use a non-slip mat under the rug as it will be slippery. Some of these mats come with perforated holes which you can use to stitch to your rug in each corner to secure.

HONEYCOMB POUFFE

Put your feet up and relax on this comfy textured pouffe. Designed as a removable cover for easy cleaning, you can easily create your own pouffe at a fraction of the cost of those on the high street with a simple rectangle of Honeycomb stitch, a piece of fabric and a bag of beans.

HOOK

8mm Tunisian hook with 40cm (16in) cable

YARN

700g Aran weight (10-ply) cotton yarn – used double throughout

OTHER MATERIALS

2m (2yd) stretch jersey fabric (the type that comes in a tube) in a colour similar to your yarn

500g bag of bean bag beans

Wool tapestry needle

4 elastic hair ties

SPECIAL STITCHES AND TECHNIQUES USED

Tunisian Simple Stitch (Tss): see Basic stitches

Tunisian Purl Stitch (Tps): see Basic stitches

FINISHED SIZE

40cm wide x 25cm high (16 x 10in)

NOTE

YARN IS USED DOUBLE THROUGHOUT THIS PATTERN.

POUFFE

Foundation Row: Ch 50. Pick up a loop from back bump in 2nd ch from hook, and in each ch to end, leaving all loops on hook. Return.

Row 2: *Tps 1, Tss 1. Repeat from * to last st, work end st. Return.

Row 3: *Tss 1, Tps 1. Repeat from * to last st, work end st. Return.

Repeat Rows 2 and 3 until work measures 100cm (40in). Bind off.

HONEYCOMB POUFFE CHART

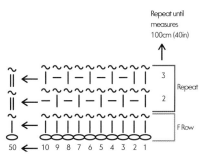

FINISHING

Stitch short ends together with mattress stitch (see Techniques) to form a tube.

Thread about 1m (1yd) of yarn onto a tapestry needle and knot one end. Insert the needle at the seam and approximately 5cm (2in) down from the top edge and make a few small stitches to secure. Make large running stitches about 5cm (2in) long all the way around, pulling up gathers as you go. You won't be able to completely close the hole yet, but gather in as much as you can. Make a few small stitches and a knot to finish off.

Turn work to the right side and re-thread your needle with more yarn. Insert the needle about 1cm (¹/₂in) from top edge, secure thread near seam with a few small stitches and rearrange gathers so that they sit neatly, make large running stitches between gathers to close up hole completely. Finish off with a few small stitches and a knot.

INNER LINING

Cut 50cm (20in) off the end of the jersey fabric and set aside for later.

Holding the longer piece of jersey fabric wrong side out, tie one of the elastic hair ties approximately 20cm (8in) down from the top edge. Tie as tightly as you can without putting too much strain on the elastic. Tie another elastic tie around the same spot.

Turn right side out and smooth out the excess fabric.

Place inner bag into pouffe, and holding the sides of the inner bag up fully, carefully start filling it with bean bag beans until you have used about ²/₃ of the bag (you will still have quite a bit of excess fabric here). Set the beans aside and tie off with an elastic tie. Try and get as close as possible to the end of the beans, pulling excess fabric up as you go.

NOTE

YOU'LL NEED TWO PEOPLE FOR THIS JOB AND THE FILLING STAGE IS BEST DONE IN A BATHTUB OR A LARGE BOX. THOSE PESKY BEANS GO EVERYWHERE!

Tie another elastic tie around the same spot.

Fold the excess fabric to one side, tucking the fabric evenly up around the sides of the pouffe.

Take the shorter piece of fabric you cut earlier and tuck it under the opening to neaten everything up.

Take a 2m (2yd) length of yarn and thread it doubled onto a tapestry needle. Leaving a long tail for tying into a bow later, make running stitches around the open edge of the crocheted piece, holding onto to the tail end as you sew. Gather up as tightly as you can and tie the two ends into a bow. There will still be a large opening but this will be hidden underneath.

NOTE

OVER TIME YOUR BEANS WILL SETTLE AND MAY REQUIRE A TOP UP.

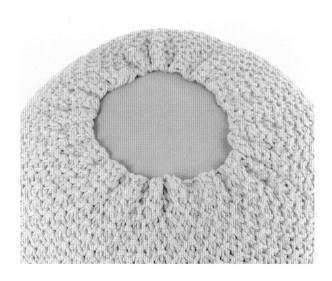

SAMPLER BLANKET

Showcase your new skills and create a beautiful keepsake with this Sampler Blanket as you practice many of the stitch patterns found within this book.

HOOK

6mm Tunisian hook with 100cm (40in) cable

5mm (US H8) regular crochet hook

YARN

Any DK (8-ply) yarn in the following colours:

A Cornflower Blue – 100g

B Mint – 100g

C Medium Pink – 100g

D Aqua – 200g

E Apricot – 100g

F Coral – 100g

G Light Blue – 100g

H Lemon – 100g

I Cerise – 100g

J Light Pink – 100g

K Green – 100g

L Lavender – 100g

M Turquoise – 100g

N Cream – 100g

SPECIAL STITCHES AND TECHNIQUES USED

Tunisian Full Stitch (Tfs): see Basic stitches

Special Tss (STss): insert hook under next vertical bar and under adjacent top horizontal bar (this gives extra stability to the Tss in eyelet rows)

Long Tunisian Front Post Double Crochet (LTfpdc): yo, insert hook under both strands of vertical bar indicated in pattern, yo and pull up lp, yo, pull through 2 lps on hook (1 lp left on hook)

Tss2tog: insert hook through next 2 vertical bars, yo and pull up a lp (1 lp on hook)

Tss3tog: insert hook through next 3 vertical bars, yo and pull up a lp (1 lp on hook)

Tss5tog: insert hook through next 5 vertical bars, yo and pull up a lp (1 lp on hook)

Bobble: yo in contrast colour, insert hook Tks-wise (through centre of front and back vertical bars), yo and pull up lp, yo and pull through 2 lps on hook, *yo, insert hook back into same sp, yo and pull up lp, yo and pull through 2 loops on hook. Repeat from * twice more, yo and pull through 4 lps on hook, yo with main colour, pull through lp just made

Carrying yarn: Wrap yarn not in use over working yarn before completing stitch approximately every 2-3 sts to end

Tunisian Slip Stitch (Tsl): pick up next vertical bar as if to Tss and leave on hook without working stitch

FINISHED SIZE

110 x 130cm (43 x 51in)

NOTE

THE FIRST ST OF EVERY ROW WILL ALWAYS BE A TSS AND IS NOT COUNTED IN THE PATTERN. THE LAST ST OF EVERY ROW, REGARDLESS OF STITCH PATTERN IS ALWAYS WORKED THE SAME AS AN END STITCH (SEE BASIC STITCHES).

BLANKET

STRIP 1 (MIXED TSS)

Foundation Row: Using Colour **A** and Tunisian hook, ch 172. Insert hook in second ch from hook, yo and pull up lp, leaving lp on hook; repeat for each ch to end (172 lps on hook). Return.

Row 2: Tss to end. Return.

Row 3: Work in Tss using Colour **A** to end. Return: join Colour **B** and work return in new colour.

Row 4: Continuing with Colour **B**, Tss to end. Return.

Row 5: Tss to end. Return: join Colour **C** and work return in new colour.

Row 6: Continuing with Colour **C**, Tss to end. Return.

Row 7: Tss to end. Return: join Colour **D** and work return in new colour.

STRIP 2 (DIAGONAL EYELET)

Row 8: Continuing with Colour **D**, work Tss to end. Return.

Row 9: Tss 2, *yo, sk next st, STss, yo and pull up lp, Tss 2. Repeat from * to end. Return.

Row 10: Tss in next st, *yo, sk next st, Tfs into next sp, Tss 2. Repeat from * up to last eyelet sp, yo, sk next st, Tfs into sp, Tss to end. Return.

Row 11: *yo, sk next st, Tfs into next sp, Tss 2. Repeat from * to last eyelet sp, yo, sk next st, Tfs into sp, Tss to end. Return.

Row 12: *Tfs into next sp, Tss 3. Repeat from * to last 3 sts, Tss to end. Return, changing to Colour **E** for last st of return pass.

STRIP 3 (GRID)

Row 13: Continuing with Colour **E**, Tss to end. Return, changing to Colour **F** on last st.

Row 14: Tss to end. Return, changing back to Colour **E** on last st.

Row 15: Tss 3, *LTfpdc around corresponding st 2 rows below (in Row 13), Tss 3. Repeat from * to end. Return, changing to Colour **G** on last st.

STRIP 4 (EYELET)

Row 16: Continuing with Colour **G**, *yo, Tss2tog. Repeat from * to end. Return, changing to Colour **H** on last 2 st.

STRIP 1

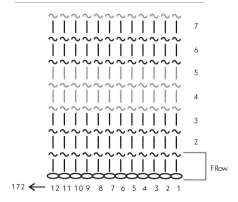

STRIP 2

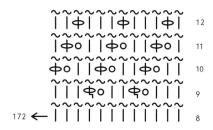

STRIP 3

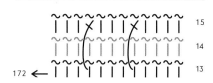

STRIP 4

STRIP 5 (STAR STITCH)

Row 17: Continuing with Colour **H**, *Tfs in next sp, Tss in next st. Repeat from * to end. Return.

Row 18: Tss to end. Return.

Row 19: Tss 3, *Tss5tog, [yo, insert hook back through same sts, yo pull up loop] twice, (5 lps back on hook), Tss 3. Repeat from * to end. Return.

Row 20: Tss to end (see note). Return, changing to Colour **G** on last st.

NOTE

TAKE CARE NOT TO MISS THE 2ND AND 4TH BARS IN STAR. THESE WILL BE SITTING BACK FROM FROM THE REST OF THE STS.

STRIP 6 (EYELET)

Row 21: Continuing with Colour **G**, *yo, Tss2tog. Repeat from * to end. Return, changing to Colour **I** on last st.

STRIP 7 (MESH STITCH)

Row 22: Continuing with Colour **I** *Tfs in next sp, Tss in next st. Repeat from * to end. Return, changing to Colour **J** on last st.

Row 23: Tfs into sp between 2nd and 3rd sts and into each sp between sts to last st, work end st. Return, changing back to Colour **I** on last st.

Row 24: Tfs into sp between 1st and 2nd sts and into each sp between sts up to last sp, sk this sp, work end st. Return, changing back to Colour **J** on last st.

Row 25: Repeat Row 23. Return, changing back to Colour **I** on last st.

Row 26: Repeat Row 24. Return, joining Colour **K** on last 2 st.

STRIP 8 (BOBBLES)

Row 27: Continuing with Colour **K**, repeat Row 23. Return without changing colour at end.

Row 28: Tss to end. Return.

Row 29: Tss to end. Return.

Row 30: Tss 8, *using Colour **L** make Bobble, using Colour **K,** Tss 8. Repeat from * to end. Return. Fasten off contrast Colour **L**.

Row 31: Continuing on with Colour **K**, Tss to end. Return, changing to Colour **M** on last st.

STRIP 9 (EYELET)

Row 32: Continuing with Colour **M**, *yo, Tss2tog. Repeat from * to end. Return, changing to Colour **N** on last st.

STRIP 5

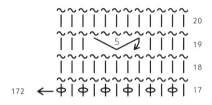

STRIP 6

STRIP 7

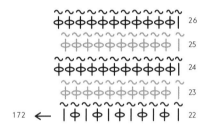

STRIP 8

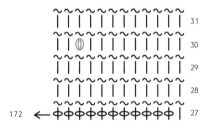

STRIP 9

STRIP 10 (HONEYCOMB STITCH)

Row 33: Continuing with Colour **N,** *Tfs into next sp, Tss into next st. Repeat from * to end. Return.

Row 34: *Tps in next st, Tss in next st. Repeat from * to end. Return.

Row 35: *Tss in next st, Tps in next st. Repeat from * to end. Return.

Row 36: Repeat Row 34, changing to Colour **M** on last st of return.

STRIP 11 (EYELET)

Row 37: Continuing with Colour **M,** *yo, Tss2tog. Repeat from * to end. Return, changing to Colour **A** on last st.

STRIP 12 (WAVE)

Row 38: Continuing with Colour **A,** *Tfs into next sp, Tss into next st. Repeat from * to end. Return.

Row 39: *Tss 2, Tdc 4, Tss 2, Tsl 2. Repeat from * to end. Return, changing to Colour **B** on last st.

Row 40: Tss to end. Return.

Row 41: Ch1, Tdc in next st, *Tss 2, Tsl 2, Tss 2, Tdc 4. Repeat from * to end, working end st as a Tdc. Return.

Row 42: Tss to end. Return, changing to Colour **C** on last st.

STRIP 13 (TSS STRIPES)

Row 43: Continuing with Colour **C,** Tss to end. Return, changing to Colour **D** on last st.

Row 44: Tss to end. Return, changing to Colour **E** on last st.

Row 45: Tss to end. Return, changing to Colour **F** on last st.

STRIP 14 (RIB)

Row 46: Continuing with Colour **F,** Tss to end. Return.

Rows 47-48: *Tps 1, Tks 1. Repeat from * to end. Return.

Row 49: Work as for rows 47-48, changing to Colour **G** on last st of return pass.

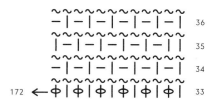

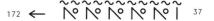

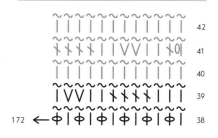

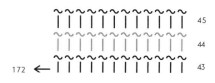

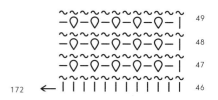

STRIP 15 (FANTAILS)

Row 50: Continuing with Colour **G**, Tss to end. Return.

Row 51: Tss to end. Return, changing to Colour **H** on last st.

Row 52: Tss 3, *Tss3tog, yo, insert hook back through same 3 sts, yo and pull lp through (3 lps back on hook). Repeat from * to last 3 sts, Tss 2, work end st. Return, changing back to Colour **G** on last st.

Row 53: Continuing with Colour **G**, Tss 3, *working into cluster sts [Tss 1, sk 1, Tss 1], Tfs into sp. Repeat from * to last 3 sts, Tss 2, work end st. Return.

Row 54: Tss to end. Return, changing to Colour **J** on last st.

STRIP 16 (ARROWHEAD STITCH)

Row 55: Continuing with Colour **J**, Tss to end. Return.

Row 56: *Tss2tog, yo. Repeat from * to last st, yo, work end st. Return.

Row 57: Tss 1, *Tfs into next sp, Tss 1. Repeat from * up to last sp, Tfs 1, work end st. Return.

Row 58: Work as for Row 56.

Row 59: Work as for Row 57, changing to Colour **K** on last st of return pass.

PATTERN REPEAT

Rows 60-64: Work as for Strip 1 starting from Row 3 and replacing colours with Colours **K** and **C**. Change to Colour **N** on last st of final return.

Rows 65-69: Work as for Strip 2 using Colour **N**. Change to Colour **A** on last st of final return.

STRIP 15

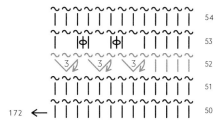

STRIP 16

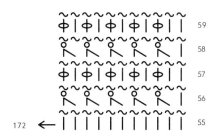

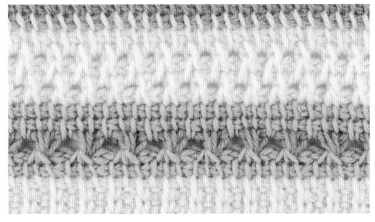

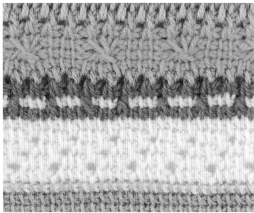

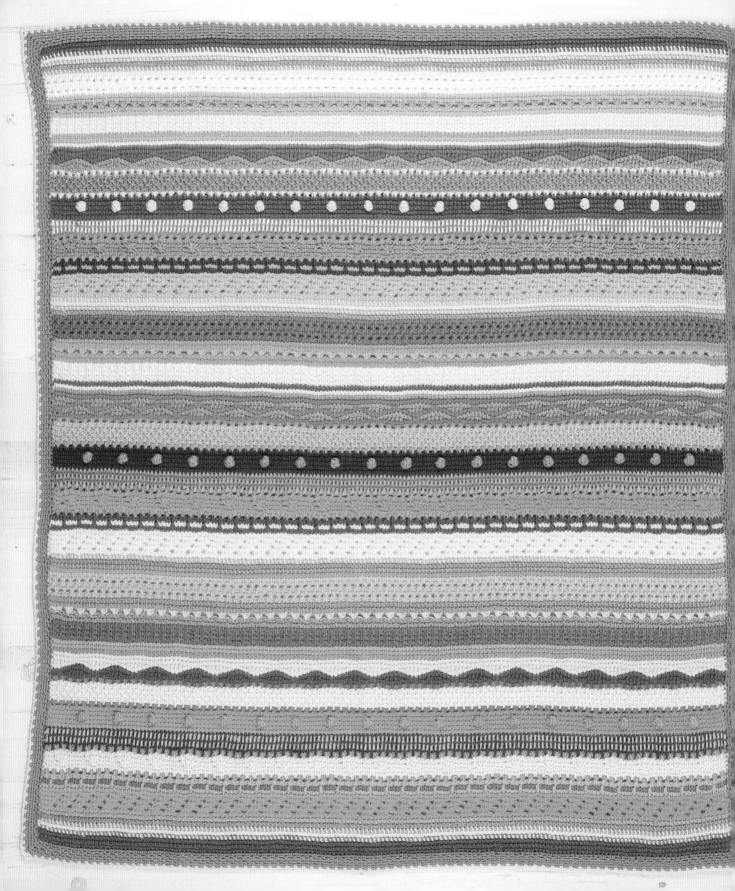

Rows 70-72: Work as for Strip 3 using Colours **A** and **B**. Change to Colour **C** on last st of final return.

Row 73: Work as for Strip 4 using Colour **C**. Change to Colour **D** on last st of final return.

Rows 74-77: Work as for Strip 5 using Colour **D**. Change to Colour **C** on last st of final return.

Row 78: Work as for Strip 6 using Colour **C**. Change to Colour **E** on last st of return.

Rows 79-83: Work as for Strip 7 using Colours **E** and **F**. Change to Colour **I** on last st of final return.

Rows 84-88: Work as for Strip 8 using Colours **I** and **G**. Change to Colour **K** on last st of final return.

Row 89: Work as for Strip 9 using Colour **K**. Change to Colour **J** on last st of return.

Rows 90-93: Work as for Strip 10 using Colour **J**. Change to Colour **K** on last st of final return.

Row 94: Work as for Strip 11 using Colour **K**. Change to Colour **M** on last st of return.

Row 95: *Tfs into next sp, Tss into next st. Repeat from * to end. Return, changing to Colour **L** on last st.

Row 96: *Tss 2, Tdc 4, Tss 2, Tsl 2. Repeat from * to end. Return, changing back to Colour **M** on last st.

Row 97: Tss to end. Return, changing back to Colour **L** on last st.

Row 98: Ch1, Tdc in next st, *Tss 2, Tsl 2, Tss 2, Tdc 4. Repeat from * to end, working last Tdc as end st. Return, changing back to Colour **M** on last st.

Row 99: Tss to end. Return, changing to Colour **C** on last st.

Rows 100-102: Work as for Strip 13 using Colours **C, B** and **A**. Change to Colour **N** on last st of final return.

Rows 103-106: Work as for Strip 14 using Colour **N**. Change to Colour **D** on last st of final return.

Rows 107-111: Work as for Strip 15 using Colours **D** and **E**. Change to Colour **F** on last st of final return.

Rows 112-116: Work as for Strip 16 using Colour **F**. Change to Colour **G** on last st of final return.

Rows 117-121: Work as for Strip 1 starting from Row 3 replacing colours with Colours **G** and **H**. Change to Colour **J** on last st of final return.

Rows 122-126: Work as for Strip 2 using Colour **J**. Change to Colour **I** on last st of final return.

Rows 127-129: Work as for Strip 3 using Colours **I** and **E**. Change to Colour **K** on last st of return.

Row 130: Work as for Strip 4 using Colour **K**. Change to Colour **L** on last st of return.

Rows 131-134: Work as for Strip 5 using Colour **L**. Change to Colour **K** on last st of final return.

Row 135: Work as for Strip 6 using Colour **K**. Change to Colour **M** on last st of return.

Rows 136-140: Work as for Strip 7 using Colours **M** and **N**. Change to Colour **A** on last st of final return.

Rows 141-145: Work as for Strip 8 using Colours **A** and **B**. Change to Colour **H** on last st of final return.

Row 146: Work as for Strip 9 using Colour **H**. Change to Colour **C** on last st of return.

Rows 147-150: Work as for Strip 10 using Colour **C**. Change to Colour **H** on last st of final return.

Row 151: Work as for Strip 11 using Colour **H**. Change to Colour **G** on last st of return.

Rows 152-156: Work as for Strip 12 using Colours **G** and **F**. Change to Colour **B** on last st of final return.

Rows 157-159: Work as for Strip 13 using Colours **B, E** and **D**. Change to Colour **H** on last st of final return.

Rows 160-163: Work as for Strip 14 using Colour **H**. Change to Colour **J** on last st of final return.

Rows 164-168: Work as for Strip 15 using Colours **H** and **L**. Change to Colour **N** on last st of final return.

Rows 169-173: Work as for Strip 16 using Colour **N**. Return.

Row 174: Tss using Colour **N**. Join Colour **C** on last st of forward pass and complete return in new colour.

Row 175: Tss to end. Return.

Row 176: Tss using Colour **C**. Join Colour **B** on last st of forward pass and complete return in new colour.

Row 177: Tss to end. Return.

Row 178: Tss using Colour **B**. Join Colour **A** on last st of forward pass and complete return in new colour.

Rows 179-180: Tss to end. Return. Bind off and weave ends in.

BORDER

NOTE
THE BORDER IS WORKED IN REGULAR CROCHET.

Change to 5mm crochet hook.

Row 1: Using Colour **D** join into any corner, 3 sc in same st (corner made), sc in each st up to next corner, 3 sc into same st. Continue working a sc into each st between corners and 3 sc into each corner. Join with a ss into first st. Don't turn.

Row 2: Ss into centre corner st, [sc, ch 2, sc] into same st, ch 1, sk 1, *sc, ch 1, sk 1. Repeat from * up to next centre corner st, [sc, ch 2, sc]. Continue working in pattern along each edge and corner to end. Join with a ss into first corner sp. Don't turn.

Rows 3-5: [sc, ch 2, sc] into corner sp, ch 1, *sc into ch-1 sp, ch 1. Repeat from * up to next centre corner st, [sc, ch 2, sc]. Continue working in pattern along each edge and corner to end. Join with a ss into first corner sp. Don't turn. Fasten off after Row 5.

Row 6: Join Colour **B**, work as for previous rows. Fasten off and weave in ends.

FINISHING

I highly recommend wet blocking your finished blanket as this will improve the drape dramatically and open up the lacy stitches.

TECHNIQUES

SLIPKNOT

Make a loop near the end of the yarn. Pull the working end of the yarn through the loop and place it onto the hook.

Pull the working end of yarn to tighten the loop on the hook.

MAGIC RING

Make a circle near the end of the yarn and hold firmly in your left hand.

Insert hook into circle and draw up a loop.

Make as many stitches as pattern says then pull tail end of yarn to tighten loop.

CHAIN

Yarn over hook and pull through loop on hook.

SLIP STITCH (SL ST)

Insert hook into stitch, yarn over and pull the yarn through both the stitch and the loop on the hook, leaving one loop on the hook.

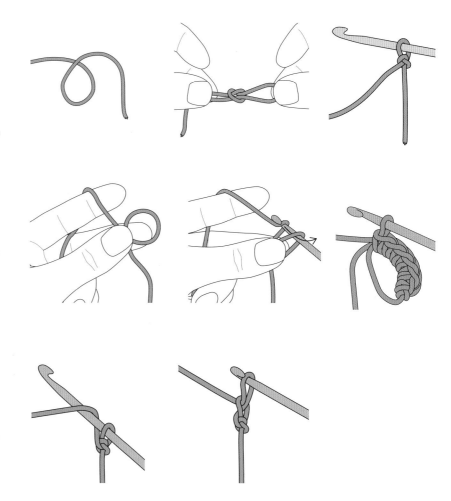

SINGLE CROCHET (SC)

Insert hook into stitch, yarn over and pull the yarn through the stitch (2 loops on hook).

Yarn over hook again and pull it through both loops on the hook.

HALF DOUBLE CROCHET (HDC)

Yarn over hook, then insert the hook into the stitch, yarn over and pull through the stitch (3 loops on hook).

Yarn over and pull the yarn through all three loops on the hook to leave one loop.

CRAB STITCH (REVERSE SINGLE CROCHET)

This stitch is worked the same as a normal sc but is worked in reverse order from left to right instead.

With the right side of work facing you, join yarn with a slip stitch into first st on left hand side, ch 1.

Insert hook from front to back into next stitch on the right.

Yarn over and draw yarn through (2 loops on hook).

Yarn over and draw through both loops on hook (crab stitch made).

Repeat steps 2-4 to end of row.

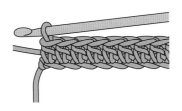

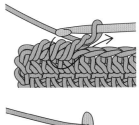

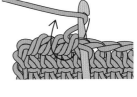

GLOSSARY

ABBREVIATIONS

ch ....chain

lp(s) ....loop(s)

st(s) ....stitch(es)

sk...........skip

sp ....space

ss ....slip stitch

m1 ....make 1

yo...........yarn over

Tss...........Tunisian Simple Stitch

STss.........Special Tunisian Simple Stitch

Tps ....Tunisian Purl Stitch

Tsl ....Tunisian Slip Stitch

Tks ....Tunisian Knit Stitch

Tfs...........Tunisian Full Stitch

Tdc ....Tunisian Double Crochet

Tfpdc......Tunisian front post double crochet

LTfpdc ....Long Tunisian Front Post Double Crochet

Tss2tog ...Decrease by working two Tss together

Tks2tog...Decrease by working two Tks together

Tss5tog ...Work five Tss stitches together

Tss3tog ...Work three Tss stitches together

Sc ....Single Crochet

Hdc ....Half Double Crochet

Sc blo .....Regular single crochet in back of loop

Trs...........Tunisian Reverse Stitch

Tes..........Tunisian Extended Stitch

CHART SYMBOLS

○	chain		+	single crochet (sc)
~	return		◍	bobble
⚇	make 1		⬯	puff
⚇	make 1 top bar (m1tb)		‖	end st
⚇	make 1 back bump (m1bb)		◠	magic ring
I	Tunisian Simple Stitch (Tss)		✳	first loop on hook
—	Tunisian Purl Stitch (Tps)		⚇	Special Tss (STss)
V	Tunisian Slip Stitch (Tsl)		⚲	Tss2tog and yarn over
♀	Tunisian Knit Stitch (Tks)		⌐	join to next triangle/square
⏀	Tunisian Full Stitch (Tfs)		⌐	join to sc
ⵟ	Tunisian Double Crochet (Tdc)		✕	crossed stitch
⎰	Tunisian front post double crochet (Tfpdc)		⋏	return (yo draw through 6 loops)
⟋	Long Tunisian Front Post Double Crochet (LTfpdc)		○	yarn over
			N	lattice stitch
⋀	decrease by working two Tss together (Tss2tog)			3 Tunisian knit stitch right cross cable
⋀	work three Tss stitches together (Tss3tog)			
5	Tss5tog and re-insert as indicated (Tss5tog)			
3	Tss3tog and re-insert as indicated			

YARN GUIDE

ENTRELAC BAG

Rico Essentials Cotton Yarn (Supplier 4): A – Denim Blue, **B** – Turquoise, **C** – Rose, **D** – Pistachio, **E** – Purple, **F** – Aquamarine, **G** – Salmon, **H** – Banana, **I** – Fuchsia, **J** – Emerald

HERRINGBONE CUSHION

Rico Essentials Cotton Yarn (Supplier 4): A – Natural, **B** – Turquoise, **C** – Grass Green, **D** – Fuchsia, **E** – Banana, **F** – Purple, **G** – Aquamarine, **H** – Salmon, **I** – Azalea

TASSEL POUCH

Drops Paris Yarn (Supplier 4):
For the Blue Pouch: **A** – Strong Blue, **B** – Light Turquoise
For the Grey and Pink Pouch: **A** – Medium Pink, **B** – Light Grey

RIBBED COWL

Drops Air Yarn (Supplier 4): Blue

OMBRE RUG

Drops Paris Yarn (Supplier 4):
A – Strong Blue, **B** – Dark Turquoise, **C** – Light Turquoise, **D** – Light Ice Blue

PINEAPPLE PINCUSHION

King Cole Cottonsoft DK Yarn (Supplier 4): A – Hot Pink, **B** – Buttercup, **C** – Lime

HONEYCOMB POUFFE

Drops Love You 5 Yarn (Supplier 4): Yellow

CHEVRON CUSHION

Moya 100% Cotton DK Harmony Yarn (Supplier 1): A – Aquamarine, **B** – Azure, **C** – Watermelon, **D** – Bubblegum, **E** – Cobalt, **F** – Denim

CHERRY POTHOLDER

Stylecraft Classique Cotton Yarn (Supplier 4): A – Greek Blue, **B** – Azure, **C** – Poppy

SIMPLE SCARF

Bendigo Woollen Mills Coloured Sock Yarn (Supplier 2): Pastel mix

Substitute yarn: The yarn used for this scarf is Australian yarn. This brand used can be shipped internationally (see Suppliers) but you may also prefer to use a substitute, in which case any sock yarn with a long colour run will work with this pattern.

GEOMETRIC WALL HANGING

Moya 100% Cotton DK Harmony Yarn (Supplier 1): A – Natural, **B** – Azure, **C** – Aquamarine, **D** – Canary, **E** – Coral

SAMPLER BLANKET

Bendigo Woollen Mills Luxury 8ply Yarn (Supplier 2): A – Bermuda, **B** – Baby Mint, **C** – Bubblegum, **D** – Aquarium, **E** – Sorbet, **F** – Lotus, **G** – Delphinium, **H** – Citrus, **I** – Cerise, **J** – Baby Blossom, **L** – Lavender, **N** – Cream

Naturally Loyal DK Yarn (Supplier 3): K – Spearmint, **M** – Aqua

Substitute yarn: The yarn used for the Sampler Blanket is Australian and New Zealand yarn. Both brands used can be shipped internationally (see supplier info) but you may also prefer to use the following budget friendly, substitute suggestion. Where possible, I have matched the colours as closely as possible except for the mint and green which didn't have a close match.

Stylecraft Special DK Yarn (Supplier 4): A – Bluebell, **B** – Spring Green, **C** – Fondant, **D** – Aspen, **E** – Apricot, **F** – Shrimp, **G** – Cloud Blue, **H** – Lemon, **I** – Fuchsia Purple, **J** – Clematis, **K** – Kelly Green, **L** – Lavender, **M** – Turquoise, **N** – Cream

SUPPLIERS

HOOKS

KNIT PRO INTERCHANGEABLE TUNISIAN HOOK

For a list of local stockists visit www.knitpro.eu

KNIT PICKS INTERCHANGEABLE TUNISIAN HOOK

Available from www.knitpicks.com

CLOVER DOUBLE-ENDED TUNISIAN HOOK

Available from www.woolwarehouse.co.uk

PONY STRAIGHT TUNISIAN HOOK (RIGID)

Available from www.woolwarehouse.co.uk

YARN

SUPPLIER 1: MOYA YARN

Many thanks to Moya Yarn and Jackie at Intambo for the generous yarn support to make the Chevron Cushion and Geometric Wall Hanging.

SUPPLIER 2: BENDIGO WOOLLEN MILLS

www.bendigowoollenmills.com.au
International shipping available

SUPPLIER 3: LITTLE WOOLLIE

www.littlewoolliemakes.com.au
Ships to Australia, New Zealand and United States

SUPPLIER 4: WOOL WAREHOUSE

www.woolwarehouse.co.uk
International shipping available

ABOUT THE AUTHOR

Michelle Robinson learnt to crochet at the age of 6 and has been hooked ever since.

With a passion for colour and fresh, modern design, Michelle strives to create beautiful but practical designs that will inspire you to break out your hooks and yarn.

Most days, Michelle can be found working from her 'creatively' messy studio under the watchful eye of her furry friend Ralph. When she's not creating you can also find her blogging at www.poppyandbliss.com or teaching Tunisian crochet workshops from her home in Melbourne, Australia, where she finds much joy and pleasure watching students gain confidence in their newfound skills.

With this book, Michelle hopes not only to inspire newcomers to the wonderful craft of Tunisian crochet but also to offer a comprehensive reference filled with lots of tips and tricks.

THANK YOU

To my loving and supportive family, especially to my partner Graham for being my rock and soothing my meltdowns when the pressure was on.

To my dear friends Shelley and Julie for always being there with a listening ear, offering encouragement, feedback and support.

To Caroline for her eagle eye, picking up on my brain fades, dotting my 'i's and crossing my 't's'.

To Maria Povh for the step-by-step photography.

To the entire team at David and Charles for giving me this wonderful opportunity, making my dream of writing a book come true and for all their hard work in making this a beautiful book.

Last but not least, thank you from the bottom of my heart to everyone who has supported my work over the years through Instagram and my blog. Without you none of this would be possible.

INDEX

A DAVID AND CHARLES BOOK
© David and Charles, Ltd 2017

David and Charles is an imprint of David and
Charles, Ltd
Suite A, Tourism House, Pynes Hill, Exeter, EX2 5WS

Text and Designs © Michelle Robinson 2017
Layout and Photography © David and Charles,
Ltd 2017

First published in the UK and USA in 2017

ISBN-13: 9781446306611 paperback
ISBN-13: 9781446375488 EPUB
ISBN-13: 9781446375495 PDF

This book has been printed on paper from
approved suppliers and made from pulp from
sustainable sources.

Printed in China through Asia Pacific Offset for:
David and Charles, Ltd
Suite A, Tourism House, Pynes Hill, Exeter, EX2 5WS

20 19 18 17 16 15 14 13 12

Content Director: Ame Verso
Acquisitions Editor: Sarah Callard
Senior Editor: Jeni Hennah
Project Editor: Caroline Voaden
Proofreader: Lynne Rowe
Design Manager: Anna Wade
Designer: Ali Stark
Art Direction and Styling: Prudence Rogers
Photographer: Jason Jenkins
Production Manager: Beverley Richardson

David and Charles publishes high-quality books on a
wide range of subjects. For more information visit www.
davidandcharles.com.

Share your makes with us on social media using
#dandcbooks and follow us on Facebook and
Instagram by searching for @dandcbooks.

Layout of the digital edition of this book may vary
depending on reader hardware and display settings.